Studies in Early Buddhist Architecture of India

Studies in Early Buddhist Architecture of India

H. Sarkar

Munshiram Manoharlal
Publishers Pvt Ltd

ISBN 81-215-0599-2
Second edition 1993

Published and printed by Munshiram Manoharlal Publishers Pvt. Ltd.
Post Box 5715, 54 Rani Jhansi Road, New Delhi 110 055.

TO
MY MOTHER

ACKNOWLEDGEMENTS

The beginning of this book can be traced back to as early as April 1961, when in a casual talk during one of his visits to the now-submerged valley, Nagarjunakonda, Shri A. Ghosh, Director General of Archaeology in India, gave me the idea – and he might not remember it—to study afresh the Buddhist architecture of Āndhra-deśa. I avail myself of this opportunity to express my gratitude and thanks to him. Being a member of the Archaeological Survey I have had the opportunity to see him and others at work and to learn consciously and unconsciously various things. I cannot, therefore, measure how much I owe to this organization and to its Director General; nor do I have words to express my gratitude to the Survey and to its individual members.

While writing the book I received constant help in various ways from my friends Shri Munishchandra Joshi, Shri B. M. Pande and Dr. M. K. Dhavalikar ; their valuable comments and suggestions gave me opportunities to reassess my standpoint time and again. For the illustrations in the book I was fortunate in getting the co-operation of Shri K. Brahmaya and Shri M. S. Mani of the Archaeological Survey. The help that I received from Shri Brijendra Prakash in the preparation of the manuscript also deserve special mention. I take here the opportunity to convey my grateful thanks to them all.

Acknowledgement is also due to the Archaeological Survey for permission to bring out the book, to publish the photographs appearing in the volume and to utilize the blocks printed on plates VIII to XII A, and XIII and figures 22, 23 and 26.

H. SARKAR

CONTENTS

LIST OF ILLUSTRATIONS

INTRODUCTION

The book presents a few studies in the development of Buddhist architecture in India from the sixth century B.C. to about the fourth century A.D. It has two main theses to advocate. Firstly, an attempt is made to show how the Buddhists adopted different types of building plans like elliptical, apsidal, circular and quadrilateral in different periods of their history. Secondly, in the opinion of the present writer, the Buddhist architecture, specially after the emergence of different sects and subsects, appears to have been influenced and conditioned by the doctrine and philosophical disposition of a particular school. For example, a sect which did not believe in the worship of Buddha could by no means have a *chaitya-gṛiha* for enshrining a Buddha-image. Similarly, a monastery with a *chaitya-gṛiha* to house an image of Buddha would speak of a definite worship of the Master in human form by its inhabitants. In some cases it is even possible to trace the gradual ideological mutation of a particular sect as well as its reaction to certain principles accepted by others. To cite an instance, one can neatly weave the history of the Apara-mahāvina-seliyas of Nagarjunakonda (Chapter V) on the basis of their architectural relics.

In the present state of archaeological research, however, it is hardly possible to reconstruct any clear picture of ideological background of various monk-settlements save a few broad indications on the changing attitudes of those sects whose identities —consequently location of their monasteries too—are known from epigraphical records. There are innumerable monasteries all over India the sectarian affiliation of which is not known, and in some cases, again, the unscientific digging has removed largely or completely all stratigraphic evidence of a settlement belonging to a particular sect. As examples of latter category Sarnath and Śrāvastī come to one's mind instantaneously. Originally both the places had settlements of the Sarvāstivādins though at Sarnath they were driven out by the Sammitīyas. Yet, the architectural remains interlocked with walls and buildings of successive phases do not give any picture of the original establishments belonging to a particular period as no attempt was made in previous excavations to correlate the structural remains with the stratigraphic data ; as a result, all important evidence relating to the development of monasteries at the above-mentioned sites is now lost. From the point of view of the present study the large-scale excavation in the Nagarjunakonda valley in Andhra Pradesh, conducted by the Archaeological Survey of India, provided an ideal opportunity, and it has been shown in Chapter V how doctrinal changes manifested themselves even in a monastic set-up. Nagarjunakonda had a unique advantage in bringing to light no less than six monasteries belonging to four different sects, each of these establishments varying from the other in details as well as in broad planning. Besides Nagarjunakonda, the only other site which provides some opportunity for taking up a similar study is the famous Buddhist site at Taxila in West Pakistan.

No generalization on the basis of architectural development is possible unless the conclusions derived from the study of these two sites find necessary corroboration from other excavated settlements; conclusions put forth in different chapters may, therefore, be taken as tentative. Yet it has to be admitted that much information in respect of ideological conflict and progressive transformation of doctrinal practices amongst different Buddhist sects can be collected also from the building plan and lay-out. Results of such studies once supplemented by available literary data are likely to cast much valuable light on the rise of different schools of thought as well as on the social and cultural environments leading to their growth. How much collective outlook of the masses and to what extent foreign ideas introduced in the trail of successive contacts contributed towards gradual metamorphosis of Buddhist ideology may also be postulated from a careful analysis of the history of Buddhist architecture: in the present studies these aspects wherever possible have duly been brought into relief.

CHAPTER ONE

THE BEGINNING

The beginning of Buddhist architecture of India is still wrapped in mist but for a few glimpses in early literature. Normally no architectural form would, however, suddenly emerge in utter disrespect to the prevalent secular or religious tradition. For instance, the practice of raising *stūpas* in some form or the other must have been in vogue even before the birth of Buddha, for burial mound is mentioned even in the Vedic literature; the *Śatapatha Brāhmaṇa* distinguishes two types of burial mounds (*śmaśāna*), viz., rectangular and circular.[1] Also the *Jātakas* refer to the building of *stūpas* on the remains of deceased persons, and probably these were earthen mounds (*mattikāthupaṁ*) like the one mentioned in the *Sujāta Jātaka.* [2] Buddha himself is said to have told Ānanda, as recorded in the *Mahāparinibbāna Sutta*, to erect *stūpa* (*thūpa*) for the Tathāgata at the four cross-roads.[3] In certain respects this practice of raising *stūpas* or sepulchral mounds had something in common with the custom of megalithic burial; in fact, the *Śatapatha Brāhmaṇa* alludes to a similar practice generally observed by the Easterners, who used to demarcate tumulus by means of indefinite number of stones.[4] This description reminds one of the megalithic stone-circles, the remains of which are found not only in peninsular India but also in the region around the Hathinia hills [5] in District Varanasi, Uttar Pradesh.

If the story of the conflict and subsequent settlement of disputes over Buddha's relics contains any truth, the Buddhists adopted the practice of raising *stūpas*, following a custom already in vogue, immediately after his death. The *Mahāparinibbāna Sutta* (VI, 62) states, 'Thus were there eight mounds (*thūpas*) for the remains, and one for the vessel, and one for the embers.' No information in respect of their construction is, however, available; perhaps these were mere earthen mounds to signify the memorials of the Great Master (below, p. 4). Had not the relics been divided, even one memorial would have sufficed to bestow due honour to the Tathāgata in the same fashion 'as men treat the remains of a king of kings'. The original idea, as it appears from Buddha's reply to Ānanda, was to raise a single *stūpa* : 'A Tathāgata, or Arahat-Buddha is worthy of a *thūpa*. A Pachcheka-Buddha is worthy of a *thūpa*.

[1] P.V. Kane, *History of Dharmaśāstra,* IV (Poona, 1953), p. 247.

[2] For other references in the *Jātakas*, see Benimadhab Barua, *Barhut,* III (Calcutta, 1937), pp. 9-11.

[3] T. W. Rhys Davids, *Buddhist Suttas,* The Sacred Books of the East, XI (Oxford, 1881), p. 93. All quotations and citing of references, unless stated otherwise, are from this Series.

[4] P.V. Kane, *op. cit.*, p. 248.

[5] A. Ghosh, ed., *Indian Archaeology 1960-61—A Review*, p. 53.

A true hearer of the Tathāgata is worthy of a *thūpa*.' That eight or ten *stūpas* were erected on the corporeal remains of Buddha was not due to any religious injunction or custom but to meet an exigency. Aśoka might have taken clue out of this emergency measure to further redistribute the relics.

Buddha's attitude towards the custom of raising *stūpas* is best revealed in his utterances in the *Mahāparinibbāna Sutta* (V, 27) when he said, 'And whosoever shall there place garlands or perfumes or paint, or make salutation there, or become in its presence calm in heart—that shall long be to them for a profit and a joy.' Whether this attitude is tantamount to worship of *stūpas* is not easy to say though one can very well trace in these words the beginning of *stūpa*-worship amongst the Buddhists. It is well known that in course of time *stūpas* became almost an embodiment of the Great Master and the idea soon developed into a cult virtually supplanting the memorial concept latent in the original practice.

When exactly the earthen tumulus assumed a durable monumental form is not known. In Vedic times bricks might have been occasionally used for enclosing the earthen mound [1], yet that can hardly be termed as a monumental form designed to survive through the ages like the ones at Bharhut, Sanchi or Bodh-Gaya. As shown in Chapter III, a permanent architectural form of the *stūpa* might have been a conscious enterprise by emperor Aśoka who is said to have constructed 84,000 *stūpas* throughout the length and breadth of his dominions (below, p. 25). At least the archaeological data known so far do not permit one to date any such remains prior to Aśoka's rule (below, p. 46); it was his Nigalisagar pillar inscription that provides for the first time an indubitable reference to the reconstruction of a *stūpa* (*Konākamanasa thube dutiyaṁ vaḍhite*).[2] Mention may be made of the fact that the word *stūpa* (*thube*) occurs here for the first time in an inscription.

In Indian epigraphs the term *chaitya* or *mahā-chaitya* has sometimes been used more or less as a synonym of a *stūpa*. The use of the term in the sense of a *stūpa* attained considerable popularity at Amaravati, Nagarjunakonda and in western India—the word *stūpa*, however, occurring in the inscriptions of Bhaja, Bedsa and Kanheri primarily to denote small-sized memorial *stūpas* raised in honour of some elder *thera*[3] fig. 11. For specifying the *stūpa*-shrines, the Buddhists there coined the word *chaitya-gṛiha* although similar structures in the Taxila region were known as *gṛiha-stūpa* (below, p. 51). The word *chaitya* or *chetiya* occurs twice in the inscriptions of Bharhut, but it is rather doubtful whether it was used in the sense of a *stūpa*, for the inscribed panels depict tree within railing as the central object. In one case two lions and six deer are shown seated round the tree with a label *Migasamadika chetiya* while in the other panel three elephants pay reverence to a tree bearing the legend *Ambode chetiyaṁ* on top.[4] Evidently, *chetiya*

[1] P.V. Kane, *op. cit.*, p. 249 f.

[2] D.C. Sircar, *Select Inscriptions bearing on Indian History and Civilization*, I (Calcutta, 1942), p. 71.

[3] Lüders' list (*Ep. Ind.* X), nos. 993, 1080-85 and 1110.

[4] Alexander Cunningham, *The Stūpa of Bharhut* (Varanasi, reprinted in 1962), p. 64.

here does not mean *stūpa*, its use being in the sense of a *vṛiksha-chaitya.* A glance through the pages of the *Mahāparinibbāna Sutta* will also bring out the difference between a *stūpa* and a *chaitya.* As a matter of fact, the former type is used there to signify funerary monuments whereas *chetiya* or *chaitya* conveys a sense very much akin to that of a shrine.[1] No less than seven *chetiyas*, viz., Chāpāla chetiya, Udena chetiya, Gotamaka chetiya, Sattambaka chetiya, Bahuputta chetiya and Sarandada chetiya at Vaiśālī and Ānanda chetiya at Bhoganagara are specifically mentioned in the *Mahāparinibbāna Sutta.* All these *chaityas* were visited by Buddha whose love for such shrines manifested itself in his famous speech on the future of the Vṛijian republic, the Lichchhavis being the most famous clan of this confederacy. Such shrines possibly did not provide any structure to stay in, as Buddha had to spend a wintry night outside at the Gotamaka chetiya (*Mahāvagga*, VIII, 13, 12).

Also there is some archaeological evidence to show that the *chaityas* mentioned above existed at Vaiśālī.[2] Two such *chaityas*, Bahuputta chaitya and Chāpāla chaitya, are depicted in one of the reliefs (pl. II A) carved on a mutilated pillar at Amaravati. These are labelled panels : one of them depicts a tree within an oblong three-barred rail with the legend *Bahaputa chetiya Vesālakāni chetiyāni* while the Chāpāla chetiya also labelled, is represented by a scene of worship of the *Buddha-pāda.* Stylistically as well as palaeographically these sculptured panels may safely be ascribed to the second century B.C. It is interesting to note that Bahuputta chaitya is shown without any structure in its vicinity.

From the scenes portrayed on the Bharhut coping stones it may appear that these *chaityas* were also basically *vṛiksha-chaityas*, the idea of which gained considerable popularity by the time the *stūpa* at Bharhut came into existence, because no less than six out of the last seven Buddha's are represented there by their trees (pl. I). The conception of *vṛiksha-chaitya* is very old dating back to the Harappan times, and when the idea of worship crept into Buddhist religion, the age-old tradition of tree-worship was also accepted by Buddha's followers. Yet, how the conception of *chaitya*-worship got mixed up with that of the *stūpa* is not clear. A perusal of the Buddhist records may show that the term *chaitya* in the sense of a *stūpa* had been used largely in the upper and the lower Deccan where, by coincidence or otherwise, the Chaityakas and their allied schools extended their sphere of influence. It is implied in the above statement that the term *chaitya* in the sense of a *stūpa* was probably introduced consciously by this school or by any of its forerunners. But it is a mere guess and need not be pressed further. At the same time it may be pointed

[1] Albert Grünwedel (tr. by Agnes C. Gibson and revised by Jas. Burgess) in *Buddhist Art in India* (London, 1901), p. 21 writes, 'Like Stūpa, the word Chaitya is applied to a monument or cenotaph, and in a secondary sense to a temple or shrine containing a *Chaitya* or *Dhātugarbha. Chaityas* or *Dagabas* are an essential feature of temples or chapels constructed for purposes of worship, there being a passage round the *Chaitya* for circumambulation *(pradakshinaya)* and from these such temples have received their appellation. The name of *Chaitya*, however, applies not only to sanctuaries but to sacred trees, holy spots, or other religious monuments.' For Ananda K. Coomaraswamy's view see his *History of Indian and Indonesian Art* (London, 1927), p. 47.

[2] A Ghosh and H. Sarkar, 'Beginnings of sculptural art in south-east India : a stele from Amaravati', *Ancient India*, no. 20, pp,. 168-79.

out that a *stūpa* within a railing, as one sees at Bharhut, Sanchi, Bodh-Gaya and Amaravati, does not differ much from the basic conception of a *vṛiksha-chaitya.* Railings are by no means a universal pattern in the *stūpa*-architecture, as they are rare in the Gandhāra region (Chapter IV) and also at Nagarjunakonda. Popularity of railings reached its climax by about the second century B.C., in the post-Mauryan epoch, when some of the most important *stūpas* like Bharhut, Sanchi, Mathurā, Sarnath, Bodh-Gaya and Amaravati were either built or enlarged. This architectural feature began even earlier, perhaps during Aśoka's time, because the mention of *silā-vigaḍa-bhīchā* in the Rummindei pillar-inscription,[1] is likely to indicate the presence of some kind of railing around the pillar installed at the place of Buddha's birth. Moreover, Sarnath brought to light an inscribed *harmikā*-rail with typical Mauryan polish.[2] All this suggests an amalgam of *chaitya* concept, in some way or the other, with the original idea of *stūpa*. Should this latter surmise prove to be nearer facts, one may as well disentangle two threads of ideas interlaced in the architectural design of a railed *stūpa*—the idea of memorial and the primitive concept of *chaitya*-worship. Both the ideas connected with this structural form must not have been accepted by Buddha as an integral part of his teachings. His attractions for *stūpas* and *chaityas* can be explained only in terms of his deep reverence to two age-old traditions which made no impact on the formulation of his doctrines. Yet, one now can easily envisage how these two traditions cast a tremendous influence in shaping the destiny of Buddhist ideology and architecture.

The concept of *Bodhi-ghara* or *Bodhi-gṛiha* appears to be the culmination of ancient *chaitya*-worship. There are innumerable sculptural representations of *Bodhi-gharas* showing several types of ground-plans (fig. 1) like circular, oblong, apsidal, octagonal etc., and with stately elevations. A detailed study of these plastic forms may prove that the development of *Bodhi-gharas* followed a distinct pattern unconnected with that of *stūpa*-worship. An inscription from Nagarjunakonda datable to the third century A.D. mentions a gift of a *Bodhi-ghara* (*Bodhi-rukha prāsādo*) to a Ceylonese monastery (*Sīhaḷa-vihāre*). Coomaraswamy[3] has collected all necessary information on *Bodhi-gharas* or structures around *Bodhi*-tree along with exhaustive illustrations (fig. 1), a perusal of which may show that these structures enclosing the tree were no less elaborate than the *stūpas*. It will not be a distortion of facts if one assumes that Buddhist architecture in India followed three main streams of ideology, viz., (i) *chaitya*-worship, culminating in the conception of *Bodhi-vṛiksha-prāsāda*, (ii) *stūpa* as memorial later symbolized the Master's aniconic representation, and (iii) the combination of both these concepts resulting into the emergence of railed *stūpas* of Bharhut, Sanchi, Amaravati etc.

In the sphere of residences for monks the change is even more phenomenal than the transformation of ideology associated with the *stūpa*-architecture. From a humble

[1] D.C. Sircar, *op. cit.*, p. 70.

[2] Daya Ram Sahni, *Guide to the Buddhist ruins of Sarnath* (Delhi, 1933), p. 4.

[3] A.K. Coomaraswamy, 'Early Indian Architecture', *Eastern Art*, II (Philadelphia, 1930), pp. 225-235.

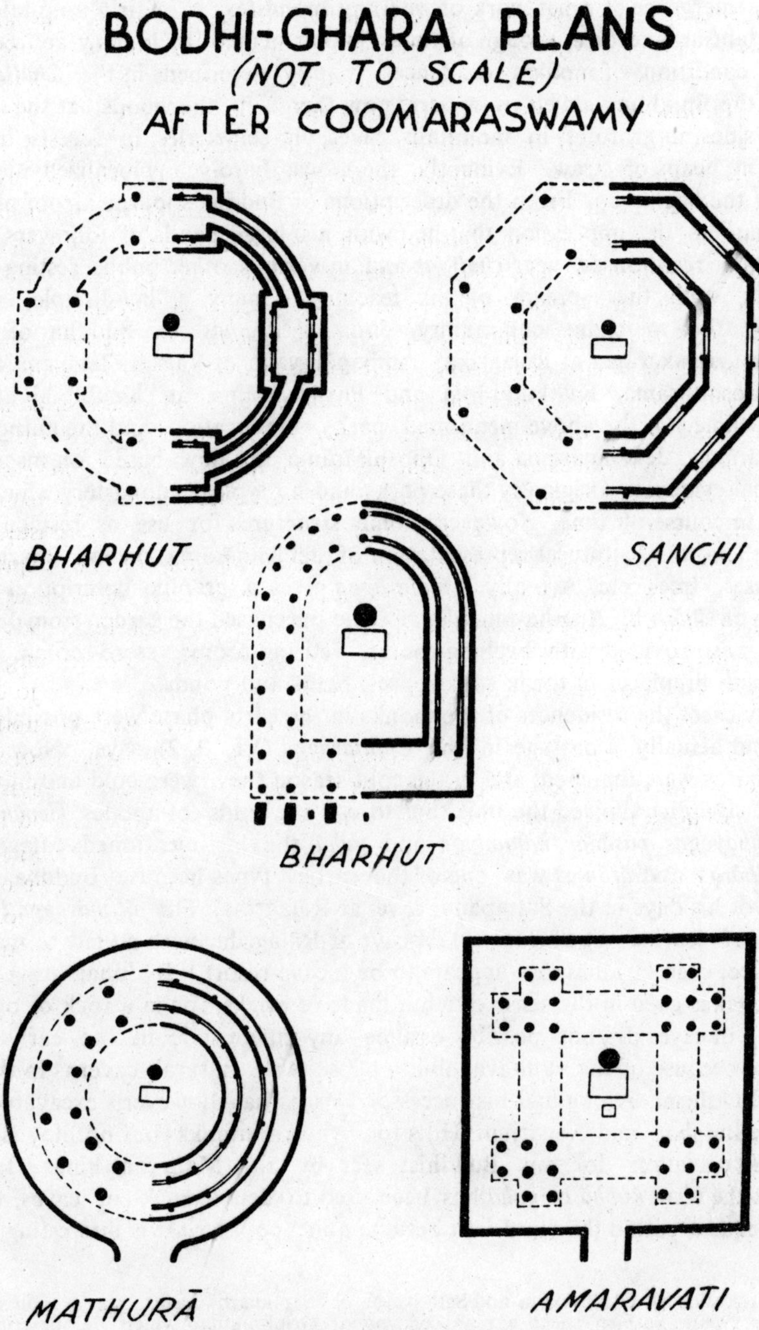
BODHI-GHARA PLANS
(NOT TO SCALE)
AFTER COOMARASWAMY
BHARHUT
SANCHI
BHARHUT
MATHURĀ
AMARAVATI

FIG, 1

thatch to the emergence of a net-work of well-knit monastery is a fairly long tale told mostly by extant architecture, though at times supplemented by literary sources too. The earliest condition of monk's residences is aptly described in the *Chullavagga* (VI, 1): 'So the Bhikkhus dwelt now here, now there—in the woods, at the foot of trees on hill-sides, in grottoes, in mountain caves, in cemeteries, in forests, in open planes, and in heaps of straw.' Evidently, there was hardly any localized monastic settlement in the beginning. From the descriptions of Buddha's journey from place to place one gathers the impression that he, with his large bands of followers, often stayed in village rest-houses, near *chaityas* and in various other public resting-places for travellers. With the spread of his teachings many a lay-disciple, mostly belonging to the merchant community, donated *ārāmas* to Buddha of which Veluvanārāma, Jīvakārāma at Rājagṛiha, Ambapāli-vana at Vaiśālī, Jetavanārāma at Śrāvastī, Ghoshitārāma, Kukkuṭārāma and Pāvāriyārāma at Kauśāmbī attained considerable fame. Of the above-mentioned parks, the location and the authenticity of the Jīvakārāma, Jetavanārāma and Ghoshitārāma are now based on inscrutable archaeological evidence. Originally these parks had no typical monastery which must have grown in course of time. However, some structures for use as residences did exist inside them: the sculptural representation of Jetavanārāma on the Bharhut rail depicts houses, trees etc. Actually *Chullavagga* gives a graphic description of the construction of *vihāra* by Anātha-piṇḍaka after he purchased the garden from Jeta, the Kumāra. It was provided with dwelling-rooms, retiring-rooms, store-rooms, service halls, halls with fireplaces in them, storehouses, baths and ponds.

In many cases the residences of the monks in the early phase were possibly made of thatch, and actually a passage in the *Chullavagga* (VI, 2, 2) says, 'Now at that time the Vihāras were thatched; and in the cold season they were cold and in the hot season hot.' Buddha allowed the Bhikkhus to use five kinds of abodes (*lenāni*), viz., *vihāras*, *aḍḍhayogas*, *pāsādas*, *hammiyas* and *guhā*, the last-mentioned category like thatched *vihāras* and *ārāmas* was one of the earliest types because Buddha himself spent some of his days in the Sattapaṇṇi cave at Rājagṛiha. The *Mahāvagga* (VI, 15, 1) mentions of clearing out of a mountain-cave at Rājagṛiha with a view to make it a dwelling-place; even Gṛidhrakūṭa appears to be a cave-resort.[1] Buddhaghosha, on the other hand, takes *guhā* in the sense of a hut made of bricks, or in a rock or of wood. But dwelling in caves did not possibly assume any magnitude in the early phase, maybe more because of the non-availability of suitable natural caverns in the early centres of Buddhism. Aśoka and his successor Daśaratha, however, excavated a few caves in the Barabar and Nagarjuni Hills for Ājīvika monks but nothing is known about cave-excavation for any Buddhist sect by the Mauryan kings. In these inscriptions the term *kubhā* or *guhā* has been used to denote rock-cut caves, whereas in the subsequent period the word *leṇa* became quite popular. It is interesting to note

[1] For identification of Gṛidhrakūṭa and Sattapaṇṇi or Saptaparṇi caves, see A Ghosh, *Rajgir* (New Delhi, 1958). Fa-hien spent a night on mount Gṛidhrakūṭa, which he described as a cavern in the rocks. See James Legge, *A record of Buddhistic Kingdoms being an account by the Chinese Monk Fa-hien of his travels in India and Ceylon (A.D. 339-414)* (Oxford, 1886), pp, 82-84.

that the use of the last-mentioned word is confined mainly to western India and Orissa, and occurs in the inscriptions from Nasik, Kanheri, Kuda, Mahad, Kol, Karle, Sailarwadi, Junnar and Karad in Maharashtra, Pabhosa near Kauśāmbī, Uttar Pradesh, and Udayagiri and Khandagiri caves in Orissa.[1] Why the term *leṇa* (also *lena* or *layana*) was preferred in these regions is hard to trace, its original meaning being only abode used generally in a wider connotation.[2] In Maharashtra it is still used to denote a cave, while *gumphā* in the sense of a rock-cut cave is widely current in Orissa. Such caves specially when enshrining a *stūpa* are sometimes mentioned in the cave-inscriptions as *selā-ghara, chetiya-ghara*[3] or *chetia-koḍhi*.

Vhiāra appears to be the most widely-accepted term in epigraphical literature as well as in Buddhist texts for denoting monastic establishment. While the use of this term is almost universal in India the word *saṅghārāma*, also frequently noticed in the inscriptions from Gandhāra and in the accounts of the Chinese travellers, is hardly used in peninsular India to signify a monastery: a Kanheri inscription, however, mentions of a *saṅghārāma*[4] which was not situated at Kanheri proper. The word *ārāma* in the sense of a park or garden occurs in the inscriptions from Mathurā, Padana and Bhattiprolu.[5]

About the prevalence of other types of abode, as stipulated by Buddha, not much information is available. The *Chullavagga* (VI, 14, 1) refers to the gift of a storeyed building (*pāsāda*) by one Visākha to the *saṅgha*. Excavations at Taxila and other places brought to light remains of storeyed monasteries; moreover, examples of cave-temples with two or three storeys at Ajanta and Ellora are well known.

Aḍḍayoga mentioned in the *Vinaya* texts is no doubt a sort of house; it is said to be a house shaped like garuḍa bird.[6] Buddhaghosha explains it as *aḍḍayoga ti suvaṇṇa Vaṅgageham* or gold-coloured Bengal house.[7] However, it appears to be a fairly big structure, bigger than a small *vihāra* although smaller than a *prāsāda* or a large *vihāra*. The *Chullavagga* (VI, 17, 1) says 'And with reference to the work on a small *vihāra*, it may be given in charge as a *navakamma* for a period of five or six years, that on an *aḍḍayoga* for a period of seven or eight years, that on a large *vihāra* or a *prāsāda* for ten or twelve years.'

1 Lüders' list. These inscriptions fall between nos. 904 and 1325.

2 For further information see, Sukumar Dutt, *Buddhist Monks and Monasteries of India* (London, 1962).

3 *Mahāvaṁsa*, XXXI, 29 defines it as *thūpaṁ tassopari gharaṁ*. The word *thupaghara* is sometimes mentioned in the Ceylonese chronicles.

4 Lüders' list. no. 988.

5 *Ibid.*, nos. 82, 973-74 and 1336.

6 R.C. Childers, *Dictionary of the Pali language* (London, 1909), p. 10.

7 *Mahāvagga*, Sacred Book of the East, XIII (Vinaya texts tr. by T.W. Rhys Davids and Hermann Oldenberg) (Delhi, 1965), p. 174n. See, however, J. Takakusu and Makoto Nagai, *Samantapāsādikā*, VI (London, 1947), p. 1215, wherein the passage reads as *supaṇṇavankaṁ gehaṁ*. Childers possibly followed this reading. Some of the tribal dormitories in Assam, with elliptical ground-plan (below, p. 24), have the appearance of a winged bird, and could not the above definition of *aḍḍayoga* find an answer in them?

Surprisingly, *hammiya* and *guhā* are excluded in the above-cited passage; possibly such edifices were not normally built or excavated, as the case may be, for use by the Buddhist monks. Now, the actual meaning of *hammiya* or *harmya* is a matter of dispute. *Amarakośa* distinguishes *harmya* from *prāsāda* by restricting the latter term to king's residences and the former to abodes of wealthy persons.[1] The word *hamma* occurs in a donative record from a cave at Kondane,[2] and *hārmya* is used in the sense of a temple in the British Museum inscription on a sculptured slab of the time of Kanishka.[3] Yet, *hammiya* of the early Buddhist texts might have been a distinct architectural tradition possessing features easily recognizable from other prevalent types. Coomaraswamy has explained *hammiya* as an open pillared pavilion with flat or domed roof while *kūṭāgāra* was a walled chamber with finials. Whatever may be the structural elevations of *hammiya* or *kūṭāgāra* the descriptions of these two types of house in the *Vinaya* texts leave no doubt as to their independent entities. In the Vedic period itself *harmya* was used in the sense of a building with stabling arrangement, the entire complex being surrounded by an enclosure.[5] Nowhere in the *Vinaya* texts – not even in the commentaries of Buddhaghosha – *hammiya* is considered as a part of other buildings. Buddhaghosha[6] describes it as *hammiyan ti upariākāsatalapatiṭṭhita kūṭāgāro pāsādo yeva,* while *pāsādo* is defined as *pāsādo ti dīghapāsādo.* Obviously, Buddhaghosha makes a distinction of *pāsāda* from *hammiya*: it is also evident from the above passage that one of the characteristics of *hammiya* was to have a *kūṭāgāra* on the topmost floor.[7] Thus *kūṭāgāra* was perhaps a part of a bigger complex and *kūṭāgāra-śālā* a building of its own type. Buddha dwelt on several occasions in a *kūṭāgāra-śālā* in the Mahāvana at Vaiśālī. The recently-discovered stele from Amaravati referred to above (p. 5) contains a fine representation of the *kūṭāgāra-śālā* of Vaiśālī. There it is depicted as an independent walled structure built right on the ground and seems to have a vaulted roof crowned by three finials. It appears to be oblong on plan with *chaitya*-façade made possibly of matted bamboo strips. On the vaulted roof is the inscription identifying the structure; the inscription reads as follow: '*Vesāliya viharati Mahāvane kuḍāgā[ra]-sālāya.*[8] And the inscription is virtually a stereotyped Buddhist phrase occurring also in the *Chullavagga*

[1] *Amarākośa*, pura-varga, kāṇḍa II, 10, ed. by Har Dutt Sharma and N.G. Sardesai (Poona, 1949), p. 76.

[2] Sukumar Dutt, *op. cit.*, p. 96

[3] Lüders' list, no. 23

[4] A.K. Coomaraswamy, 'Early Indian Architecture : III. Palaces', *Eastern Art*, III (Philadelphia, 1931), p. 193.

[5] A.A. Macdonald and A.B. Keith, *Vedic index of names and subjects*, II (Delhi, reprinted in 1958), pp. 499-500.

[6] J. Takakusu and Makoto Nagai, *op. cit.*

[7] Moti Chandra in his 'Architectural data in Jain Canonical Literature', *The Journal of the United Province Historical Society*, XXII (Lucknow, 1949), p. 47 says, '*Prāsāda* itself is explained as a long building of several storeys, or, if with a *kuṭagara* on the sky floor the term *hammiya* is applicable.'

[8] A Ghosh and H. Sarkar, *op. cit.*

(V. 13, 2, 13) as well as in the *Dīgha Nikāya* and other texts : Buddhaghosha[1] wrote a commentary on this very sentence which runs as *Vesāliyaṁ viharati Mahāvane kūṭāgāra-sālayan*. Again, there are a few sculptural representations in the aforesaid stele which depict *kūṭāgāra* on a very high platform supported by lofty wooden pillars or poles (pl. II B); such houses, as the reliefs show, could be approached only by means of long stair-case supported by three-barred railings. Perhaps these were the same as *hammiyas* of the early Buddhist texts—some sort of a pile dwelling or houses on platform still used by some of the aboriginal tribes like the Garos and the Lhota Nagas.[2] Temporary field-houses also follow basically the same structural pattern. It may be mentioned here that Buddha allowed the Bhikkhus to make houses on raised platform (*chayo*) (*Chullavagga*, V, 11, 6). Such halls have not been described as *hammiyas* but all such evidence is likely to indicate that constructing houses on high pillars or basement was possibly a common practice in that period.

If these primitive types, as mentioned above, are taken as precursor of *hammiya* or *harmya* its developed form can be seen in certain plastic representations from Bharhut or Sanchi. For instance, pl. III B presents the picture of a building with its upper storey built on rows of columns. This type of edifices need not be classed with that of a *prāsāda*, the typical example of which is provided by the labelled representation of the three-storeyed *Vejayanta prāsāda* (pl. III A) of the Bharhut relief. It appears from Buddhaghosha's commentary that a *prāsāda* should have more than two storeys, otherwise there is hardly any justification in defining it as *dīgha pāsāda* : this characteristic was not possibly shared by *hammiyas* or *harmyas*, specially in the early period. A comparison of the *Vejayanta pāsāda* (pl. III A) with *hammiya* or the pillared mansion (pl. III B) described above may bring out the following differences between the two classes of buildings.—

(i) *Prāsāda* had more than two storeys while *harmya* was only a double-storeyed house.

(ii) The upper storey of *harmya* comprised one or more *kūṭāgāras* which may be absent in case of *prāsāda*.

(iii) The ground floor of *harmya* was an open pillared-hall but that of *prāsāda* almost a closed storey meant for residential use.

(iv) For approach to the upper storey of *harmya* one had to make use of stair-case similar to the one depicted in the Amaravati relief (pl. II B) while in case of *prāsāda* all the storeys from the ground floor onwards were connected possibly with each other by flights of steps not visible from outside.

[1] *Sumangala-Vilāsini*, ed. by T.W. Rhys Davids and J. Estlin Carpenter (London. 1886), p. 309.

[2] J. H. Hutton in his introduction on J.P. Mills's *The Lhota Nagas* (London, 1922), p. XXX writes, 'In building, again, while the Angamis, Tangkhuls, Semas and other tribes south of them build on the ground, the Aos and other tribes to the north build on a bamboo platform or "machan." The Lhota method is a sort of compromise, as when he builds on a "machan" he covers the floor with "earth". The Lhotas build their granaries (*Osung*) on posts above the ground while their Bachelor's House (*Morung*) is raised about two feet above the ground on posts.' The Bhuiya dormitories are also a kind of pile-house. See S.C. Roy, *The Hill Bhuiyas of Orissa* (Ranchi, 1935). For pile dwelling amongst the Garos, see A. Playfair, *The Garos* (London, 1909).

In the absence of labelled sculpture and definite literary evidence one may very well dispute the present identification of *harmya* or *hammiya* with a building-tradition which developed out of pile-houses. Yet, there is hardly any reason to doubt open-pillared mansions with *kūṭāgāra* on the top—whatever may be its accepted name—as a type quite distinct from that of a *prāsāda*. There is another aspect of the interpretation of the term *hammiya* or *harmya*; it is well known that the name *harmikā* is derived from *harmya*. In the *Divyāvadāna* it is explained as 'a little structure on the stupa.'[1] A question naturally comes in mind: why a memorial *stūpa* was to be surmounted by a small edifice ? Theoretically speaking, earlier *stūpas* should not have it on top; in fact, one of the Sanchi reliefs[2] depicts a Brahmanical *stūpa* without any *harmikā* on the top (pl. IV A). Likewise the *stūpas* carved on a freize in the façade of the Lomas Rishi caves[3] do not also show any such motif (pl. IV B). In the circumstances one may presume that *harmikā*, as the crowning member of the *stūpas*, came into vogue at a date when a synthesis of the memorial concept with the idea of Buddha's abode had taken place. At Amravati the latter motif is represented singly by the *kūṭāgāra-śālā* of Vaiśālī (pl. II A). Further, an interesting feature of the Amaravati art, as revealed by the newly-discovered stele, is the depiction of several scenes from Vaiśālī which have hardly any parallel in the art of Bharhut or Sanchi. Buddhaghosha's commentary on the *kūṭāgāra-śālā* of Vaiśālī also reveals the importance of this structure where Buddha stayed on several occasions. This emphasis on Vaiśālī as well as on the *kūṭāgrā-śālā* situated thereat is likely to throw light on the origin of *harmikā*. Perhaps in an early phase this sacred abode of Buddha, like a temple of god, was glorified to such an extent that Buddhists took it as the symbol of the Master and adopted it as a feature distinguishing the Buddhist variety of *stūpa* from the rest. It is well known that the Mahāsāṅghikas had their earliest stronghold at Vaiśālī, and that this sect from the very beginning extended its sphere of influence more towards the south than in the north. Does it mean that it was this sect which was responsible for laying emphasis on Vaiśālī episodes and that the earliest Buddhist settlement at Amaravati sprang up as a result of their southward expansion? Time has not come to put forth such a theory but available data do indicate some such trends in the development of Buddhist ideology and architectural conceptions. As a corollary to the above hypothesis one may as well postulate that the idea of *harmikā* might have evolved out of the famous *kūṭāgāra-śāla* of Vaiśālī. The idea might have come into existence by about Aśoka's time, for Sarnath, as already pointed out, yielded a monolithic *harmikā*-rail with typical Mauryan polish. All these hypotheses do not by any means explain the reasons for the use of the term *harmikā* since the *kūṭāgāra-śālā* of Vaiśālī was a structure on the ground and not a house built on piles

1 A.K. Coomaraswamy 'Indian Architectural Terms', *Journal of American Oriental Society*, 48 (New Haven, 1928), p. 258.

2 Marshall and others, *Monuments of Sanchi*, II (Calcutta), pl. LII-23.

3 Maulvi Muhammad Hamid Kuraishi, *List of Ancient Monuments, Protected under, Act VII of 1904 in the province of Bihar and Orissa* (Calcutta, 1931), p. 37.

or platform ; the reason for the use of this term may, however, be sought in its actual location which, like a *hammiya*,stood, as it were, on a raised pile.

Buddha allowed the monks to use all the above-mentioned types of dwellings either as temporary residences or as rain-retreats (*vasā-vāsa*) which may or may not have been full-fledged *vihāras*, with ownership belonging to the *saṅgha* of four directions whether present or to come. In the beginning, *vihāras* were possibly without any specific architectural pattern; perhaps they were exclusive residences of wandering Buddhist monks and built more often than not by lay-devotees. In the circumstances, Buddhists could hardly evolve any special type of architecture of their own. As a matter of fact, they only made use of the prevalent forms either religious or secular in character. While the former comprised *stūpas* and *chaityas*, the latter included temporary residences of monks like *pāsāda, hammiya, aḍḍhayoga, guhā, kūṭāgāra-śālā, paṇṇa-kuṭi* or *paṇṇa-śālā*, etc. Quite naturally, all these structures could not have been built invariably of permanent materials. This is apparent also from a description in the *Chullavagga* (VI, 1, 10)[1] wherein it is stated that Buddha permitted the use of five kinds of roofing materials (*pañcha chhadanāni*), viz., coverings of brick (*iṭṭakachhadanaṁ*), stone (*silā*), stucco (*sudhā*), grass (*tiṇa*) and leaf (*paṇṇa*). It may be pointed out here that Buddha often stayed in the hermitage in the Migadaya (*Mahāvagga*, VIII. 14, 11); such huts must have been very similar to those depicted on the bas-reliefs of Bharhut and Sanchi. That houses were built of bricks also may be gathered from the tailor's episode in the *Chullavagga* (VI, 5, 1). Further, excavations at Jivakārāma disclosed an array of rubble-built elliptical halls datable to Buddha's life-time. If the plastic representations of *hammiya* and *kūṭāgāra-śālā* in the aforesaid reliefs from Amaravati and other places are faithful copies of those prevalent during Buddha's time, or even subsequent to that, thatched vaulted roof may be taken as a very common type of the period. Of the five kinds of dwellings, *hammiya, aḍḍayoga* and some *vihāras* had possibly thatched roofs, walls being made either of mud or wattle and daub.

There are reasons to believe that different types of structures used by the monks were basically secular buildings. Even the elliptical halls at Rajgir without any individual room or cell were simple community halls possibly modelled on the line of tribal dormitory (below, p. 24). In course of further development these monk-residences, specially the *vihāras*, were provided with stores, baths, privies, wells, tanks, etc. Even the walls were plastered and also sometimes painted with designs of wreaths, creepers and so on; imaginative drawings, however, did not find Buddha's approval (*Chullavagga*, VI, 3, 2).

Whatever may be the process of development towards increasing comforts and refinements, the building traditions as depicted in the Buddhist texts and, also to certain extent, in the *Jātakas*, show hardly any individuality of their own. In fact, the Buddhists made use of various architectural forms like the *stūpas*, the *vṛiksha-chaityas*, the railing and several types of dwellings prevalent during the period from

1 Bhikkhu J. Kashyap, ed., *The Chullavagga* (Nālandā-Devanāgarī-Pali Series, 1956). p. 248.

Buddha to Aśoka's coming to power. The basic architectural types were, therefore, only continuation of earlier traditions, though at times modified or embellished according to new circumstances. This trend almost remained unaltered till the time of Aśoka when several changes revolutionized the Buddhist architectural conceptions by introducing many novel features and new structural forms, the details of some of which are discussed in Chapter III.

CHAPTER TWO

ELLIPTICAL STRUCTURES

Elliptical structures of ancient India are not widely known and the general absence of their reference in leading books on ancient Indian architecture may even cast a doubt as to their very existence. But elliptical structures corresponding to a linear plan with semicircular ends [1] did exist, and as will be shown presently, this constructional form, despite its exiguity in India, appears to be a very old idea, possibly older, at least archaeologically, than the circular and apsidal ones.

Structures with truly oval or elliptical ground-plan are, however, extremely rare in India. Hence Coomaraswamy's statement that 'an oval plan is unknown to Indian architecture'[2] is not very wide of the mark for, with the probable exception of the Lomas Rishi cave, no structure with truly elliptical plan has so far come to light.

Generally scholars have described the cella of the Lomas Rishi cave (fig. 3) in the Barabar Hill as circular, or more precisely, an incomplete circle. It does not appear to be an unfinished cave so far as the ground-plan is concerned inasmuch as the wall of the cella though not polished bears a smoothed surface.[3] In all likelihood it was intended to be an oval shrine (longer axis 17 ft. or 5·2 m. and shorter axis 14 ft. or 4·3 m.) used as a place of worship by the Ājīvikas. Yet, this is the only example of truly oval ground-plan in India and it answers correctly to the description of *kukkuṭa-aṇḍa-sadṛiśa* as given in some southern texts.

No less than half-a-dozen ancient sites, viz., Rajgir, Gopika or Nagarjuni cave, Besnagar, Nagari, Kauśāmbī and Śrāvastī have produced evidence of linear structure with semicircular extremities; for the sake of convenience such structures will be referred to in these pages as elliptical. Perhaps this form of ground-plan is referred to in the southern texts as *vṛittāyata*.

The majority of the above-mentioned sites, viz., Rajgir, Gopika cave, Śrāvastī and Kauśāmbī are confined to the Ganga basin which seems to be the cradle of this type

1 Such structures have already been described as elliptical by D. R. Bhandarkar and other excavators. For reference, see below, pp. 21 ff.

2 Ananda K. Coomaraswamy (1928), *op. cit.*, p. 259. He also thinks that P. K. Acharya in his *Indian Architecture according to the Mānasāra-śilpaśāstra* and in *A Dictionary of Hindu Architecture* refers to the term oval, perhaps meaning apsidal. The *Śilparatna* and other southern texts mentioned oval or elliptical form as *vṛittāyata* or *kukkuṭa-aṇḍa-sadṛiśa*. Information from Shri K.R. Srinivasan, Superintendent, Archaeological Survey of India.

3 M.M. Hamid Kuraishi, *op. cit.*, p. 36. He describes the cave as follows: 'The whole interior of the circular room has been left rough, and both the floor and roof of the outer apartment remain unfinished, and while the straight walls of this latter apartment are polished, the curving outer wall of the circular room is only smoothed—not polished.'

of architectural plan. With the exception of the Gopika cave in the Nagarjuni Hill all of them are attributed to the Buddhists. But the elliptical shrines of Besnagar and Nagari, both being in central India, belonged to some Vaishṇava sect; a Buddhist cave at Kolvi in Madhya Pradesh is, however, described as a long ovoid cave measuring 21 ft. ×16 ft.[1] (6·4×4·9 m.).

The earliest elliptical structures appear to be the Jīvakāmravana monastery at Rajgir, built by the famous physician Jīvaka in Buddha's life-time: the archaeological excavations at the very site revealed a monastic complex (fig. 2) comprising a few rectangular and elliptical halls.[2] At least two phases of building activity were noticed there, both being associated with elliptical halls. That these were used as halls may be affirmed from the occurrence of two openings on one side in at least three cases. As already indicated, the builders there tried to achieve the elliptical form simply by making both the ends pronouncedly convex, the longer sides being almost parallel to each other.

The ruins of rubble-built structures at the site of the Jīvakārāma are considerably old, perhaps older than any monastery hitherto unearthed in India. The coarse red ware, which the site yielded in plenty, appears to be the same as that of Period I at Rajgir of Ghosh's chronology[3], and, as such, may be dated to pre-N.B.P. period (earlier than the fifth century B.C.). Another excavation at Rajgir[4] also established the chronological priority of coarse red ware over the Northern Black Polished Ware. Hence the site, inclusive of the elliptical halls, may be dated to *circa* sixth-fifth century B.C.[5] It is interesting to record that neither any *stūpa* nor any shrine seemed to have existed at the place.

Next in order, both geographically as well as chronologically, comes the Gopika or Nagarjuni cave (fig. 3) in the Nagarjuni Hill, District Gaya, Bihar, ascribable to the third century B.C., as it bears the dedicatory inscription of Daśaratha, a Maurya king. Unlike Sudama (fig. 3) or Lomas Rishi (fig. 3) caves in the Barabar Hill it has no separate cella; consisting mainly of a single hall the cave measures 46 ft. 5 in. ×19 ft. 2 in. (14·15×6·3 m.) and is entered by a passage in the middle.[6] In plan the rock-cut chamber, without any pillar, resembles very much the elliptical halls at Rajgir. The vaulted roof of the Gopika cave rises to 10 ft. 6 in. (3·2 m.) at the centre and the entire structure was probably a rock-cut replica of a thatched or wooden building then

---

1 E. Impey, 'Description of the caves of Koolvee, in Malawa', *The Journal of the Bombay Branch of the Royal Asiatic Society*, V (Bombay, 1857), p. 344.

2 *Indian Archaeology 1954-55—A Review*, pp. 16-17; also *ibid., 1958-59*, p. 13.

3 A. Ghosh, 'Rajgir 1950', *Ancient India*, no. 7 (1951), p. 71.

4 *Indian Archaeology 1953-54—A Review*, p. 9.

5 Should it mean that the Northern Black Polished Ware, generally abbreviated as the N.B.P. Ware, did not make its appearance there during the life-time of Buddha? The characteristic Ware is now dated to *circa* sixth century B.C. to second century B.C. As full report on this excavation is not available as yet, conclusions regarding the date of the structure may be taken as tentative.

6 Alexander Cunningham, *Four Reports made during the years 1862-63-64-65*, Archaeological Survey Report, I (Simla, 1871), p. 48. Also, A.L. Basham, *History and Doctrines of the Ājīvikas* (London, 1951), pp. 154 ff.

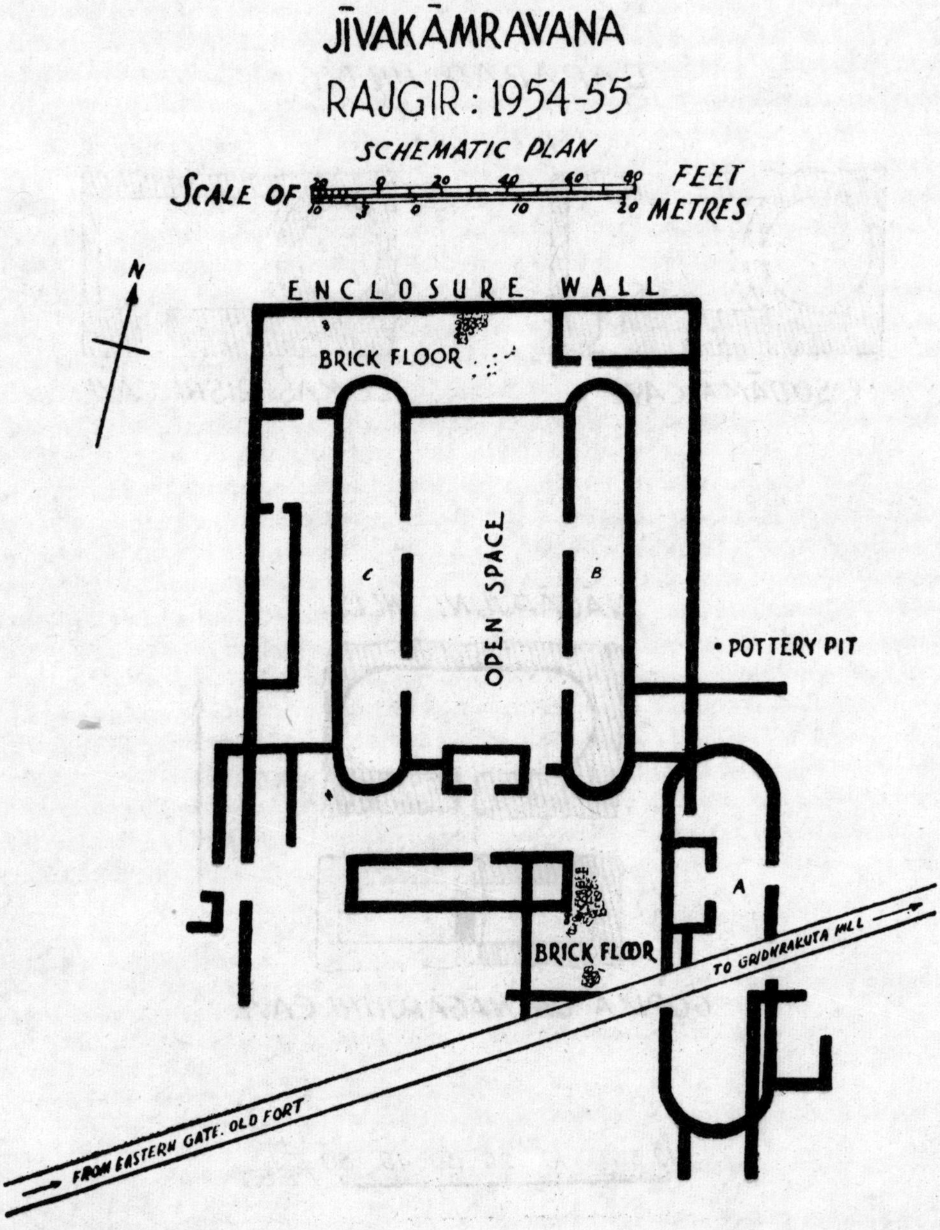
JĪVAKĀMRAVANA
RAJGIR : 1954-55
SCHEMATIC PLAN
SCALE OF
FEET
METRES
N
ENCLOSURE WALL
BRICK FLOOR
C
OPEN SPACE
B
• POTTERY PIT
A
BRICK FLOOR
TO GRIDHRAKUTA HILL
FROM EASTERN GATE. OLD FORT

FIG. 2

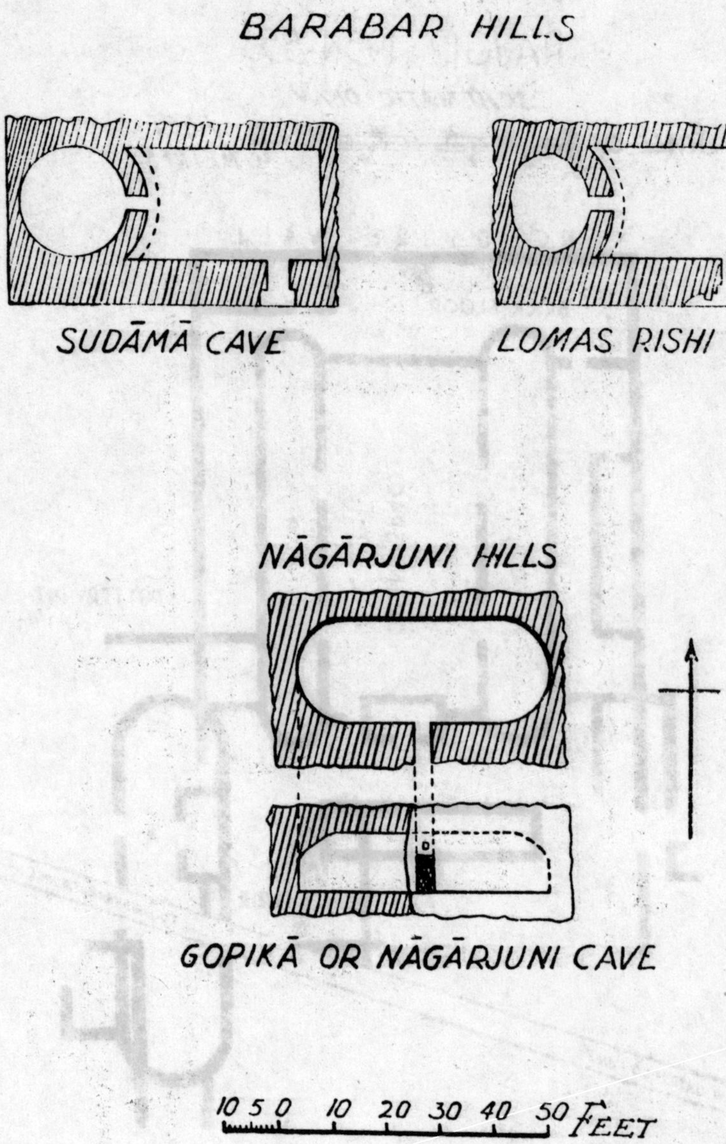
BARABAR HILLS
SUDĀMĀ CAVE
LOMAS RISHI CAVE
NĀGĀRJUNI HILLS
GOPIKĀ OR NĀGĀRJUNI CAVE
10 5 0 10 20 30 40 50 FEET

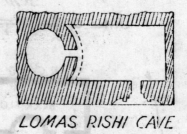

FIG. 3

in vogue. From the design of the cave-roof one may also visualize the picture of the roof[1] of the Rajgir halls.

Like the Jīvakāmravana monastery at Rajgir the Ghositārāma at Kauśāmbī is said to have been built by the merchant Ghosita during the life-time of Buddha. An inscription[2] of the first century A.D. discovered by G.R. Sharma gives the correct location of the monastery which remained continuously under occupation from *circa* sixth century B.C. to the sixth century A.D.[3] To fix correctly the date of the elliptical structure which stood on an oblong platform is, however, difficult until the final report on the excavation is published. Here also the elliptical structure followed a plan very much similar to the Rajgir halls and the Gopika cave.

The elliptical structure at Kauśāmbī (fig. 4) was made of brick and might have been a *stūpa*. Yet this is not the only elliptical structure in brick as the mound known as Pakki-kuti at the modern village of Maheth embracing a part of ancient Śrāvastī, also yielded a similar monument (fig. 5).[4] Unlike Kauśāmbī it had a central projection, or some sort of a passage, on the east, a characteristic noticed also in the case of circular *stūpa*-shrines (below, p. 26) and Vaishṇavite elliptical temples (below, p. 20). But for the central passage the example from Śrāvastī did not differ much from that of Kauśāmbī. Both of the structures were built on high platforms divided into several squares, and as usual the western side of the ellipse in either case was almost straight. The method of constructing platform by dividing it into several compartments was meant for economizing materials, a principle followed also in the case of wheel-shaped *stūpas*.[5] Such technique marked a phase of constructional advancement over the earlier method of solid brick constructions of *stūpas* or platforms. *Stūpas* with wheel-shaped plan must have come into existence in the Gandhāra[6] and Mathurā[7] regions by about the first century A.D., and it is but natural that the principle followed in case of circular constructions would also be adopted in the same period for building platforms similar to those of Kauśāmbī and Śrāvastī; consequently, the present writer is inclined to date the elliptical structures at both the sites to about the first-second century A.D.[8]

1 It appears from N.V. Mallaya's *Studies in Sanskrit Texts on Temple Architecture (with specia reference to Tantrasamuccaya)*, pp. 68-69 that like apsidal shrines the elliptical structures *(vrittāyata)* too had roofs shaped like the back of an elephant *(gajaprishṭhākāra)*.

2 A. Ghosh, 'Buddhist Inscriptions from Kauśāmbī', *Epigraphia Indica*, XXXIV, pt. I (1961), pp. 14-16.

3 *Indian Archaeology 1955-56 – A Review*, pp. 20-21.

4 J. Ph. Vogel, 'Excavations at Saheth-Maheth', *Annual Report of the Archaeological Survey of India, 1907-08* (Calcutta, 1911), pp. 108-09; also pl. XXVIII.

5 H. Sarkar, 'Some aspects of the Buddhist monuments at Nagarjunakonda', *Ancient India*, no. 16 (1960), pp. 78-82.

6 Sir John Marshall, *Taxila* (Cambridge, 1956), III, pl. 45. The example from Sirkap is only a variant of this type of *stūpa*.

7 Vincent A. Smith, *The Jaina Stupa and other Antiquities of Mathura* (Allahabad, 1901), pl. III.

8 This type of platform-construction in temple-architecture gained wide currency during the Gupta period.

This architectural form, as already stated, was accepted by the followers of Brāhmaṇical faith; the shape of the ellipse, however, did not alter in the least. As early as 1918 Bhandarkar [1] discovered an elliptical shrine, also enclosed by an elliptical wall, at Nagari, District Chitorgarh, Rajasthan: inscriptions from nearby sites, some

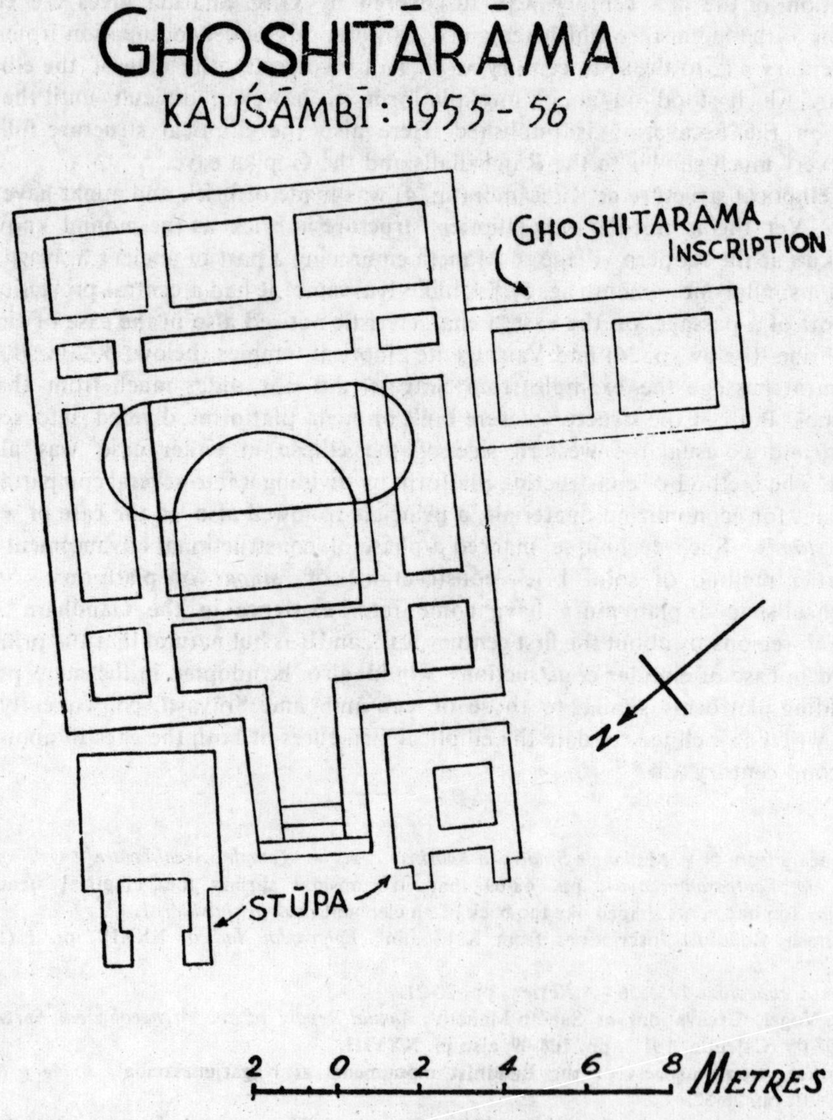

FIG. 4

[1] D.R. Bhandarkar, *The Archaeological Remains and Excavations at Nagari*, Memoirs of the Archaeologieal Survey of India, no. 4 (Calcutta, 1920), pp. 131 ff., pl. XVIII.

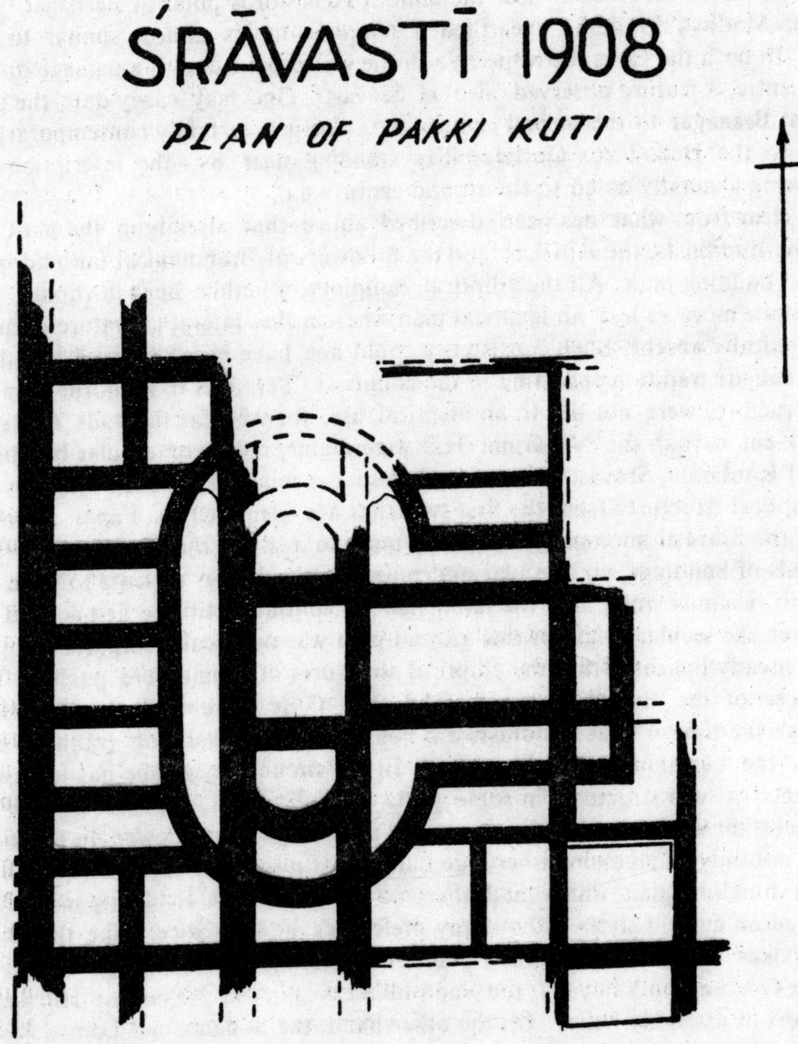

ŚRĀVASTĪ 1908
PLAN OF PAKKI KUTI
10 0 10 20 30 40 50 FEET

FIG. 5

of them dating back to the second century B.C., suggest its Vaishṇava affiliation. Again, the recent excavations near the famous Heliodoros pillar at Besnagar,[1] District Vidisha, Madhya Pradesh, unearthed a temple-complex almost similar to that of Nagari. In both the cases the respective shrine was provided with a passage or a porch in the centre, a feature observed also at Śrāvastī. One may easily date the elliptical shrine at Besnagar to the second century B.C., for it is certainly contemporary, if not earlier, to the Heliodoros Garuda-pillar standing near by—the inscription on the pillar being generally dated to the second century B.C.

It is clear from what has been described above that already in the pre-Christian times the Buddhists, the Ājīvikas and the followers of Brahmaṇical faith adopted the elliptical building plan. All the elliptical buildings, whether built in rubble, brick or rock, show more or less an identical plan wherein the lateral curvature of an ellipse was practically absent. Such consistency could not have been observed had there not been a definite tradition persisting in the country.[2] Yet, it is to be borne in mind that these structures were not put to an identical use, for whereas the halls at Rajgir and the rock-cut cave in the Nagarjuni Hill were mainly copies of secular building plan, those of Kauśāmbī, Śrāvastī, Nagari and Besnagar might have been religious shrines. The elliptical structures from the first two sites are identified as *stūpas* although the plan of the Śrāvastī monument conforms more to a shrine than *stūpa* proper. Of the two kinds of buildings, viz., secular and religious, the former appears to have evolved earlier to religious ones, and the latter had its continuity till the first-second century A.D. when the secular origin of this ground-plan was practically forgotten.

It is already indicated that the elliptical structures of Rajgir were possibly used as residences of the Buddhist monks, and that these were built by Jīvaka during Buddha's life-time. That Buddhists did not evolve any building tradition of their own in the beginning is fairly certain. In the circumstances one has to assume the prevalence of such structures in some parts of India even prior to Buddha's time. The fact that both the Buddhists as well as the Ājīvikas followed an identical plan speaks not only of a common heritage but also of a sense of catholicity in the selection of building plan which had then no religious bias. Evidently both the sects depended on current styles without any preference or prejudice. Like the Buddhists the Ājīvikas too had their regular places for meetings known as the Ājīvika *sabhā*,[3] and the Gopika, the Vahiyaka, the Vadathika caves in the Nagarjuni Hill served as some sort of assembly halls. On the other hand, the Sudama and Lomas Rishi caves with circular or oval inner chambers might have been sanctuaries modelled like Buddhist *stūpa*-shrines. As both the doctrines believed in some form of corporate ideals it is but natural that necessity of such halls, used either as residences or as

1 *Indian Archaeology 1964-65—A Review* (in the press).

2 The tradition possibly continued in south India till late medieval times as the Ranganāthasvāmī temple at Srirangam, District Thiruchchirapalli, the Jarāhareśvara temple at Kanchipuram, District Chingleput and Kaḷḷalagar temple at Aḷagarkovil near Madurai, all being in Madras State, have elliptical ground-plans. Information Shri K.R. Srinivasan.

3 A. L. Basham, *op cit.*, pp. 115-16.

assembly halls, should be felt by the either sect. All this presupposes the existence in pre-Buddhistic times of a building tradition suited to communal purposes. Unfortunately no archaeological remains of any secular building comparable to the elliptical halls, and also attributable chronologically to pre-Buddhistic period, have so far come to light. Some very important evidence is, however, available in the primitive architecture, specially among the Naga tribes of north-east frontier. For instance,

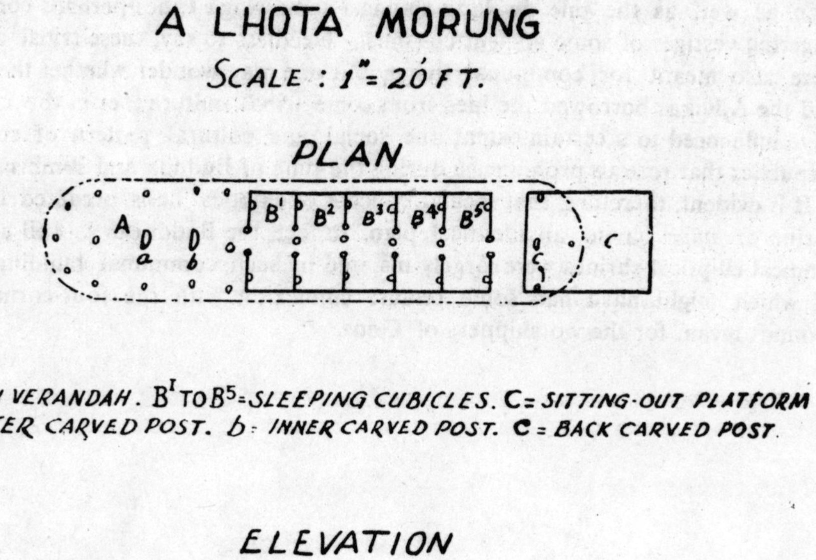

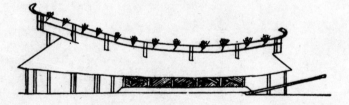

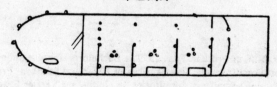

FIG. 6

the Bachelor's House (*Morung*) of the Lhota Nagas[1] (fig. 6) conforms exactly to the elliptical plan of Rajgir or Gopika cave: houses with semicircular front are also common amongst the Sema and the Lhota Nagas. Whether the Lhota dormitories should be considered as survival of an old tradition is difficult to say but the presence of pile dwelling there, old traces of which are preserved in the plastic representations from Amaravati and in some Buddhist literature[2] leads one to believe that elliptical plan as well as the pile dwelling amongst some Naga tribes perhaps constitute the lingering vestiges of some ancient customs. Needless to say, these tribal dormitories were also meant for communal living, and one may wonder whether the Buddhists and the Ājīvikas borrowed the idea from some tribal culture; even the latter might have influenced to a certain extent the social and cultural pattern of some of the Republics that rose to prominence during the time of Buddha and Bimbisāra.

It is evident, therefore, that secular concept of elliptical halls predated that of the shrine or *stūpa* having an identical plan. In fact, the Buddhists as well as the Brahmanical elliptical shrines were largely inspired by such communal building, the plan of which might have had some remote connexion with the four-cornered burial-mounds meant for the worshippers of Gods.[3]

1 J. P. Mills, *op. cit.*, pp. 24 ff. and pl. facing p. 25. The Bachelor's House is an institution common to most of the tribes in north-east frontier. Several tribes of Bihar and Madhya Pradesh follow the same custom. For distribution of village dormitories in India, see Verrier Elwin, *The Muria and their Ghotul* (Oxford, 1947), pp. 269 ff.

2 A. Ghosh and H. Sarkar, *op. cit.*, pp. 168-79. Also, see above, p. 11

3 P. V. Kane, *op. cit.*, IV, p. 247.

CHAPTER THREE

THE STUPA-SHRINES

The Buddhists in India introduced several architectural forms, of which the *stūpa*, representing a structural dome, attained maximum importance in ancient times. This well-known form, besides the rock-cut caves and the free-standing pillars, owed much of their popularity to Aśoka, who is said to have set up such monuments throughout the length and breadth of his empire. Even the *gṛiha-stūpas* or the *chetiya-gharas* possibly made their appearance during Aśoka's time. Such chapels of circular and apsidal forms seem to represent a further stage in the development of the *stūpa* cult—a development not only in the realm of architecture but also possibly in the sphere of ideology—for the *chaitya-gṛihas* or *gṛiha-stūpas* combine in themselves the memorial aspect of the *chaitya* with the concept of shrine, the latter being inseparably connected with the ideas of *bhakti* and worship, at least in the sense in which these terms are now used.

The *gṛiha-stūpa*, as the name itself suggests, is an edifice enshrining the *stūpa*, evidently of the size proportionate to the dimension of the building. So far as the archaeological remains are concerned these Buddhist shrines conform mainly to three different shapes, viz., (1) circular (2) apsidal and other cognate forms and (3) quadrilateral. It is, however, not known for certain whether elliptical form was ever connected with the *stūpa*-shrines.

1. CIRCULAR

The circular form of religious building, at first possibly copied from circular huts of primitive character, came into vogue during the Maurya rule. Of the two very early examples, the Sudama cave (fig. 3) in the Barabar Hills was meant for the Ājīvikas, while the other one (fig. 7) at Bairat,[1] a structural temple built of brick and timber, appears to have had a Buddhist affiliation. Only bits of the *stūpa*-plan have survived at Bairat, still the occurrence of a stone umbrella bearing the typical Mauryan polish would prove the existence of a *stūpa* within the circular structure, and also Aśoka as its builder. Around the *stūpa* was constructed a circular wall made of 'panels of brick work alternating with octagonal columns of wood.' The other example of brick-built circular *stūpa*-chapel (pl. V A) in somewhat better state of preservation is the one unearthed at Salihundam, District Srikakulam, Andhra Pradesh; several subsidiary shrines of identical shape also exist there.[2] In both the cases at

[1] Daya Ram Sahni, *Archaeological Remains and Excavations at Bairat,* pp. 28-32.

[2] A. Ghosh, ed., *Archaeological Remains Monuments and Museums* (New Delhi, 1964), pl. XXVIII.

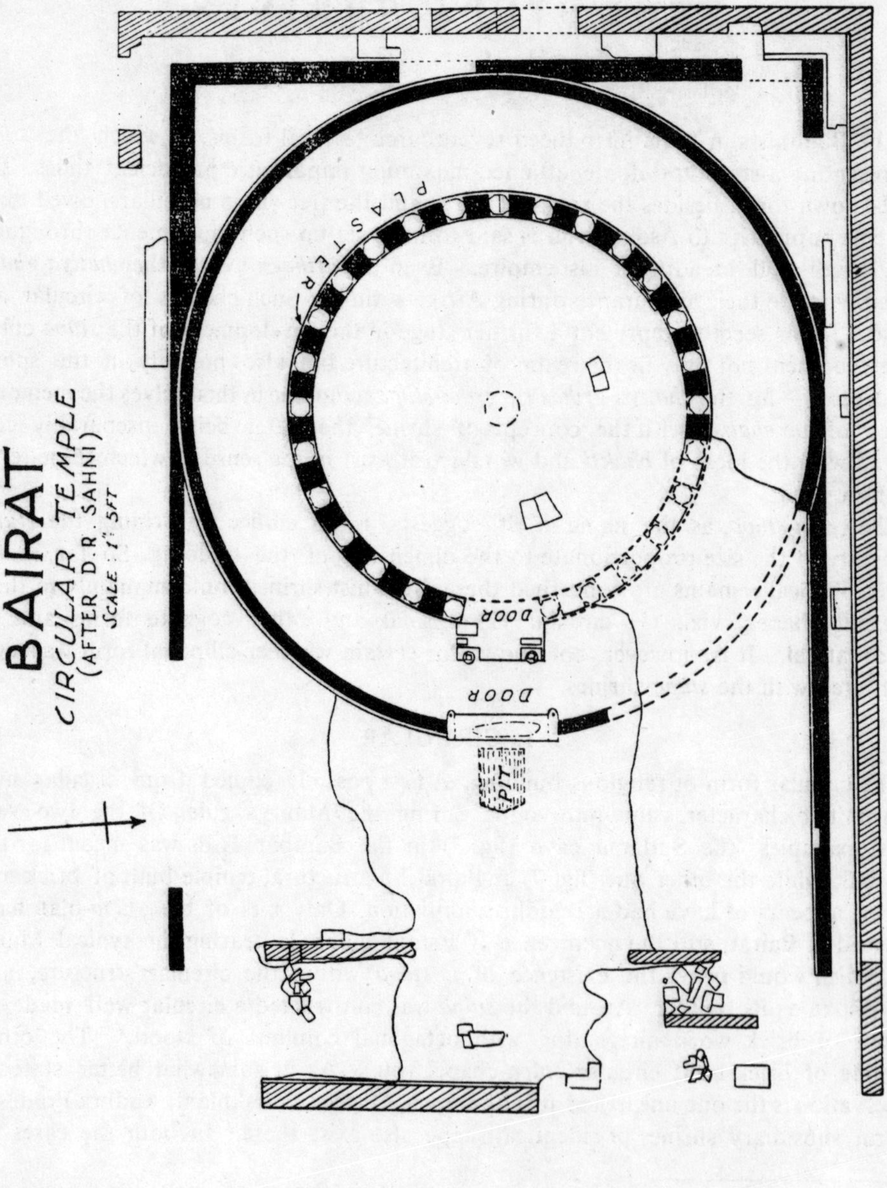
BAIRAT
CIRCULAR TEMPLE
(AFTER D R SAHNI)
SCALE 1"=5FT
PLASTER
DOOR
DOOR
PIT

FIG. 7

Salihundam the circular shrine of second-first century B.C. was to be approached by a narrow passage and this feature, common also to some elliptical buildings (above, p. 19), had its beginning already at Bairat (fig. 7).

Besides these structural temples in brick,[1] there are at least three rock-cut examples, two of them being located on the Western Ghats while the other in the Nallamalai Range of the Eastern Ghats. The circular example (fig. 8) of the Tulaja-*leṇa* group at Junnar, with a diameter of 25 ft. 6 in. (7·8 m.) resembles very much the circular temple at Bairat: instead of octagonal wooden pillars the *stūpa* in the former cave is encircled by a row of stone columns, also octagonal in cross-section. This feature is absent both at Guntapalli in the Nallamalai Range, District Krishna, Andhra Pradesh, as well as at Kondavite near Bombay. In front of the Guntapalli cave, datable to the second century B.C., is a vestibule of roughly crescentic ground-plan—a thin wall separating it from the circular shrine having a ribbed vaulted roof (pl. VII A). At Kondavite the circular plan (fig. 8) is similar to that of Guntapalli but here a narrow opening connects the *stūpa*-shrine with the rectangular vestibule. In other words the cave-temple at Kondavite follows a ground-plan very similar to the Sudama or Lomas Rishi caves (fig. 3) in the Barabar Hill. Cave 13 of Pitalkhora[2] (fig. 9) is also nearer to the apsidal form but for the circular end of the ground plan. It is pillared, and the form seems to have been influenced by the development of apsidal temples. Mention may be made here of the occurrence of a simple type of circular *stūpa*-chamber at Bhaja and Bedsa as reported by Fergusson and Burgess.[3]

Thus it appears that circular *stūpa*-shrines came into use quite early in the history of Buddhist architecture. Aśoka was perhaps responsible for giving this structural form a religious status but the source of his inspiration is not easy to ascertain. In primitive architecture its use seems to be fairly widespread,[4] yet no definite proof as to the borrowings of circular building-plan from that direction is available but for the fact that the Guntapalli cave (pl. VII A) practically copied the primitive circular huts of Andhra Pradesh. The Bairat (fig. 7) and the Junnar (fig. 8) examples, for that matter are evolved circular structures and might not have been copied directly from the aboriginal prototypes. On the other hand, a striking similarity of the plan of Bairat and Junnar with the circular peripteral temple of Greece[5] may cast a doubt on the theory of indigenous origin of this building-plan. Nonetheless, the basic plan of such

[1] A circular *gṛiha-stūpa* in brick appears to have been discovered at Kondapur, a Sātavāhana site in Andhra Pradesh, but the traces of the excavated ruins are now so much disturbed that no definite conclusion could be arrived at.

[2] M. N. Deshpande, 'The Rock-cut caves of Pitalkhora', *Ancient India*, no. 15 (1959), pp. 66-93.

[3] James Fergusson and James Burgess, *The Cave Temples of India* (London, 1880), pp. 228-29.

[4] Circular huts are still common in the coastal Andhra Pradesh and also to certain extent in the desert districts of Rajasthan, in eastern Ladakh and certain parts of Saurashtra. (Information from H. K. Rakshit of Anthropological Survey of India). Of the aboriginal tribes, the Chenchus, the Yanadis, the Todas, the Birhors and the Hill-Pantarams use circular huts. Even now the granaries in many parts of India are built on circular plan. There are several representations of circular huts on the sculptures from Bharhut, Sanchi, Amaravati and Nagarjunakonda.

[5] Banister Fletcher, *A History of Architecture* (London, 1961) pp. 108-109.

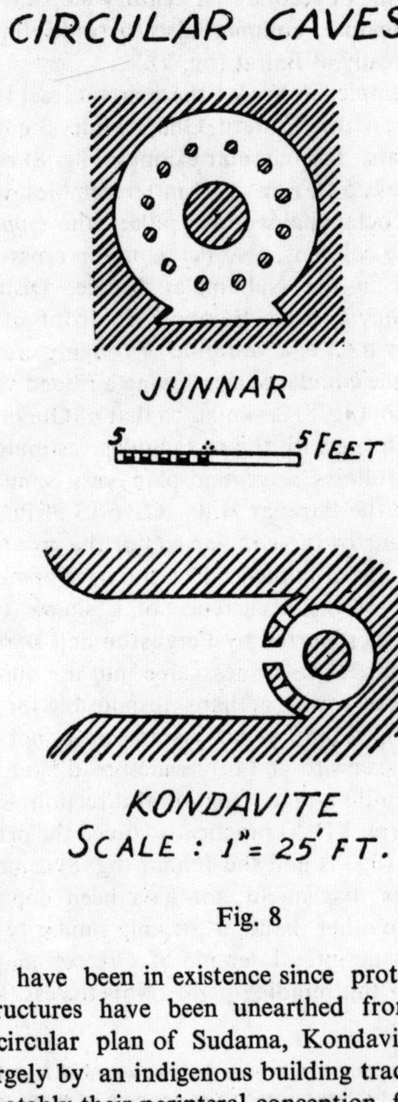

Fig. 8

circular edifices must have been in existence since protohistoric times as remains of circular huts or structures have been unearthed from sites like Navdatoli and Tekkalakota.[1] The circular plan of Sudama, Kondavite and Guntapalli caves was possibly inspired largely by an indigenous building tradition but the examples from Bairat and Junnar, notably their peripteral conception, form a distinct group imbibed with a much developed architectural vision. Again, the chronological gap between Bairat and Junnar eliminates the possibility of the latter being influenced directly by the tradition that evolved at the former site. Exchange of ideas and wide contact during the Maurya period might have been, therefore, responsible for assimilation of peripteral conception from some foreign source, and the circular plan of the Bairat

1 *Indian Archaeology 1957-58—A Review*, pl. XXXII C. For Tekkalakota see M. S. Nagaraja Rao, *The Stone Age Hill Dwellers of Tekkalakota*, (Poona, 1965), p. 15, fig. 6.

temple seems to be an outcome of such fusion. On the other hand, the rock-cut example of the Tulaja-*leṇa* derived the same architectural tradition from some other source[1] in the wake of tradal contact during the first century A.D. It is interesting to recall that some Śaka and *Yavana* donors participated in the excavation of Junnar group of caves (see Lüders' nos., 1154, 1156 and 1162).

The evolution of the circular Buddhist shrines took a slightly different turn at Nagarjunakonda (Chapter V) where, though such *gṛiha-stūpas* in the true sense of the term were absent, the circular form assumed a certain new functional role. At least on one occasion the circular structure enshrined possibly the image of Buddha but in some other cases it was used as the residences of the leading monks. Structurally also these shrines showed certain modifications. For example, the passage, as one finds at Salihundam, was replaced at Site 27 of Nagarjunakonda (pl. VIII B) by a flight of steps flanked on both the sides by the bas-reliefs of *purṇa-ghaṭa*. Moreover, those used as cells for the monks had their interior square instead of circular. Also, as stated above, the *gṛiha-stūpas* of circular variety was transformed like those of the apsidal shrines into image-chapels. As the date of Site 27 is the eleventh regnal year of Rudrapurushadatta, the last known Ikshvāku king, the excavated remains may very well be dated to the beginning of the fourth century A.D. An interesting fact which needs emphasis is the use of the circular chamber as residence, a practice hardly followed in case of apsidal shrines.[2] This may be due to local influence as circular huts are quite common in this part of Andhra Pradesh, the area being also inhabited by the Chenchus using circular dwellings of varying dimensions.

2. APSIDAL

From the very beginning the apsidal structures in India were intimately associated with the Buddhist religious practices. It has hardly any primitive or protohistoric parallel in India: but to imagine that the Buddhists developed it out of nothing would rather be a difficult assumption. The shape though quite common in the civil architecture of ancient Palestine and in different cultures that flourished in the Mediterranean region has seldom been met with in any protohistoric sites here. Even the aboriginal population has rarely made use of this building plan. But the Kaura caste of Orissa[3], speaking the Telugu language, builds wall-less mat-huts with an apsidal ground plan: certain nomadic tribes of Andhra Pradesh and Mysore also use such huts invariably with an open front. It has to be admitted that the evidence of survival enumerated above is too scanty to justify the existence of a distinct building tradition with an apsidal ground plan in ancient or protohistoric India.[4] In such

1 The circular peripteral temple of Vesta, Tivoli (B.C. 27-A.D. 14) had its cella about 24 ft. diameter, surrounded by a peristyle of 18 pillars (Fletcher, *op. cit.*, p. 194).

2 At Bedsa monastic cells are arranged around an apsidal court.

3 N.K. Bose, *Peasant life in India : a study in Indian Unity and Diversity,* Memoir of Anthropological Survey of India, no. 8 (Calcutta, 1961), pp. 14-15.

4 N.R. Banerjee in *The Iron Age in India* (Delhi, 1965), p. 18, refers to an apsidal structure of dressed stones from Period II (*circa* 500-200 B.C.) of Ujjain. Its purpose, however, is not known.

circumstances one has to postulate a theory of independent origin of such structural form or take it as a case of borrowing from some other culture. Before examining the question it is worth while to make a rapid survey of different types of apsidal shrines and their line of development.

According to the shape of an apse, which term normally includes both semi-circular as well as polygonal form, the apsidal *gṛiha-stūpas* in India may be divided into three main groups (fig. 9) viz., apse in the form of a (i) semi-circle, (ii) an octagon and (iii) apse formed by a row of pillars within an oblong plan. By far the largest number of caves and structures fall within the first group, whereas the other two categories are represented by one or two localized specimens. For instance, octagonal apse was confined only to Taxila while there are only two examples—one from Ajanta (cave 10) and the other from Aurangabad (cave 4)[1]—of apse formed by a row of pillars within a rectangular ground-plan. Of the semi-circular type, the cave 13 of Pitalkhora stands as a unique example with a much pronounced circular end.

The apsidal *stūpa*-shrines embrace comparatively a wider area of distribution than the circular ones in spite of the fact that both the varieties originated practically in the same period. Harwan[2] in Kashmir and Brahmagiri,[3] Chitaldrug District, Mysore, are respectively the northernmost and the southernmost limits of distribution of apsidal monuments No apsidal temple is known to have been found to the east of Rajgir[4] in Bihar and Udayagiri[5], District Puri, Orissa, and on the west beyond Taxila.[6] Its highest concentration is in western India where, with few exceptions,[7] all the examples are carved out of rock. On the other hand, there is hardly any rock-cut apsidal *chaitya-gṛiha* on the east coast: surprisingly, this form did not attain much popularity in the Ganga basin, the cradle of Buddhist culture.

Broadly the apsidal *stūpa*-shrines may be divided into two major groups from the point of view of constructional material, viz., (i) structural and (ii) rock-cut, the latter being also largely conditioned by the geographical distribution of tractable rocks in India. In archaeological records the structural tradition may claim slight chronological priority over the rock-cut ones, for the temple 40 at Sanchi[8] (fig. 10) and an apsidal

[1] James Burgess, *Report on the Antiquities in the Bidar and Aurangabad Districts*, Archaeological Survey of Western India, III (London, 1878), pl. XL, 3.

[2] Ram Chandra Kak, *Ancient Monuments of Kashmir* (London, 1933), pp. 108-111 and pl. LXXVII.

[3] R.E.M. Wheeler, 'Brahmagiri and Chandravalli 1947: megalithic and other cultures in the Chitaldrug District, Mysore State' *Ancient India*, no. 4 (1947-48), p. 186.

[4] Its ruins can be seen near the famous Muniyar Math. An apsidal structure of unknown religious affiliation is reported from Ahichchhatra.

[5] *Indian Archaeology 1958-59—A Review*, pp. 38-40.

[6] Sir John Marshall, *Taxila* (Cambridge, 1951), I, pp. 151-54.

[7] The living temple at Ter, District Osmanabad, Maharashtra, is one such exception. Originally it might have been a Buddhist apsidal shrine, later converted into a Vaishṇava temple. An apsidal brick-built temple ascribable to the medieval period has been recently exposed at Devnimori, District Sabar-Kantha, Gujarat. See *Indian Archaeology, 1960-61—A Review*.

[8] Sir John Marshall and others, *op. cit.*, I, pp. 66 ff.

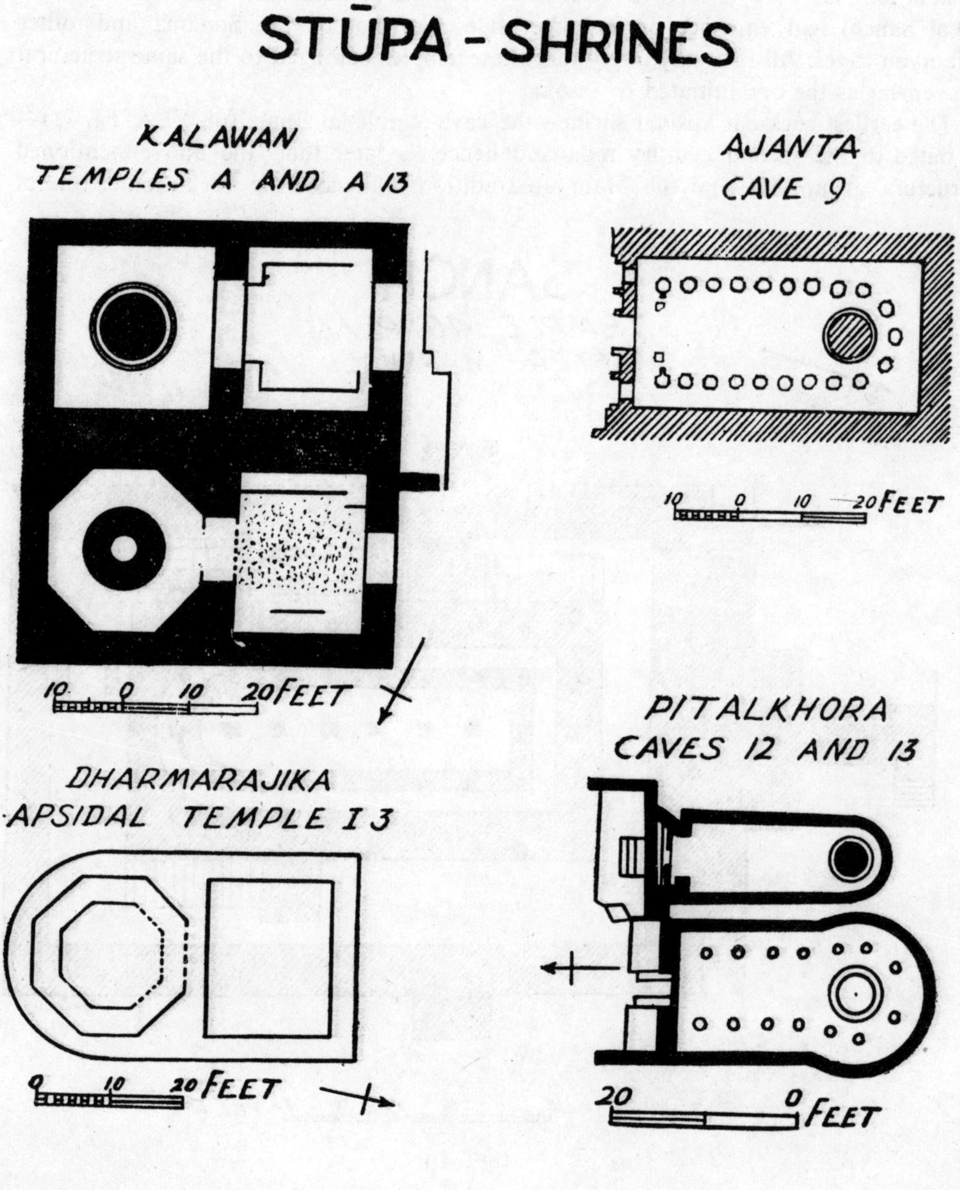
STŪPA - SHRINES
KALAWAN
TEMPLES A AND A 13
10 0 10 20 FEET
AJANTA
CAVE 9
10 0 10 20 FEET
DHARMARAJIKA
APSIDAL TEMPLE I 3
0 10 20 FEET
PITALKHORA
CAVES 12 AND 13
20 0 FEET

FIG. 9

structure from Sarnath[1] are generally attributed to the late Mauryan period; the remains of a rubble-built *chaitya-gṛiha* at Rajgir discovered below the Muniyar Math is likely to go back to the same epoch. Both at Sanchi and Sarnath the ruins of apsidal temples were unearthed close to an Aśokan column, and further, the temple 40 at Sanchi had entrance on its longer sides like that of the Sudama and other Mauryan caves. All this may imply that these temples belonged to the same structural movement as the one initiated by Aśoka.

The earliest rock-cut apsidal shrine—the cave-temple at Bhaja (pl. VI A; fig. 11)—is dated to the second century B.C., and hence, is later than the above-mentioned structural group. How far the Mauryan tradition influenced the rock-architecture of

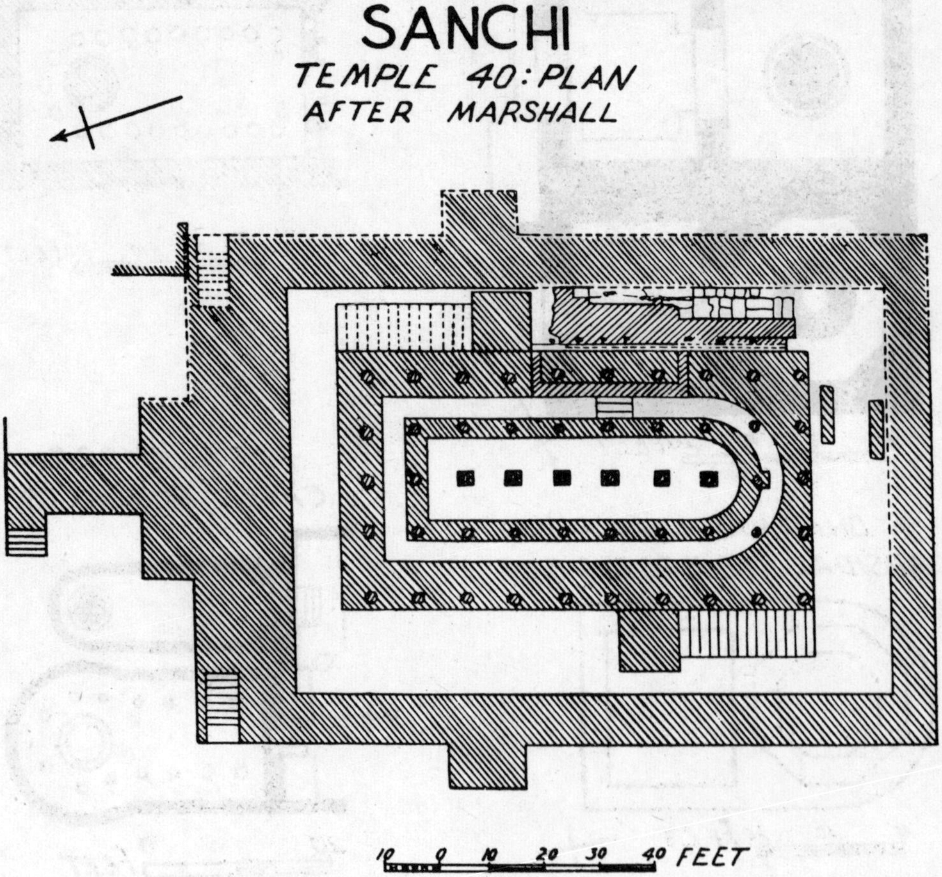

FIG. 10

[1] *Annual Report of the Archaeological Survey of India 1914-15* (Calcutta, 1920), p. 109.

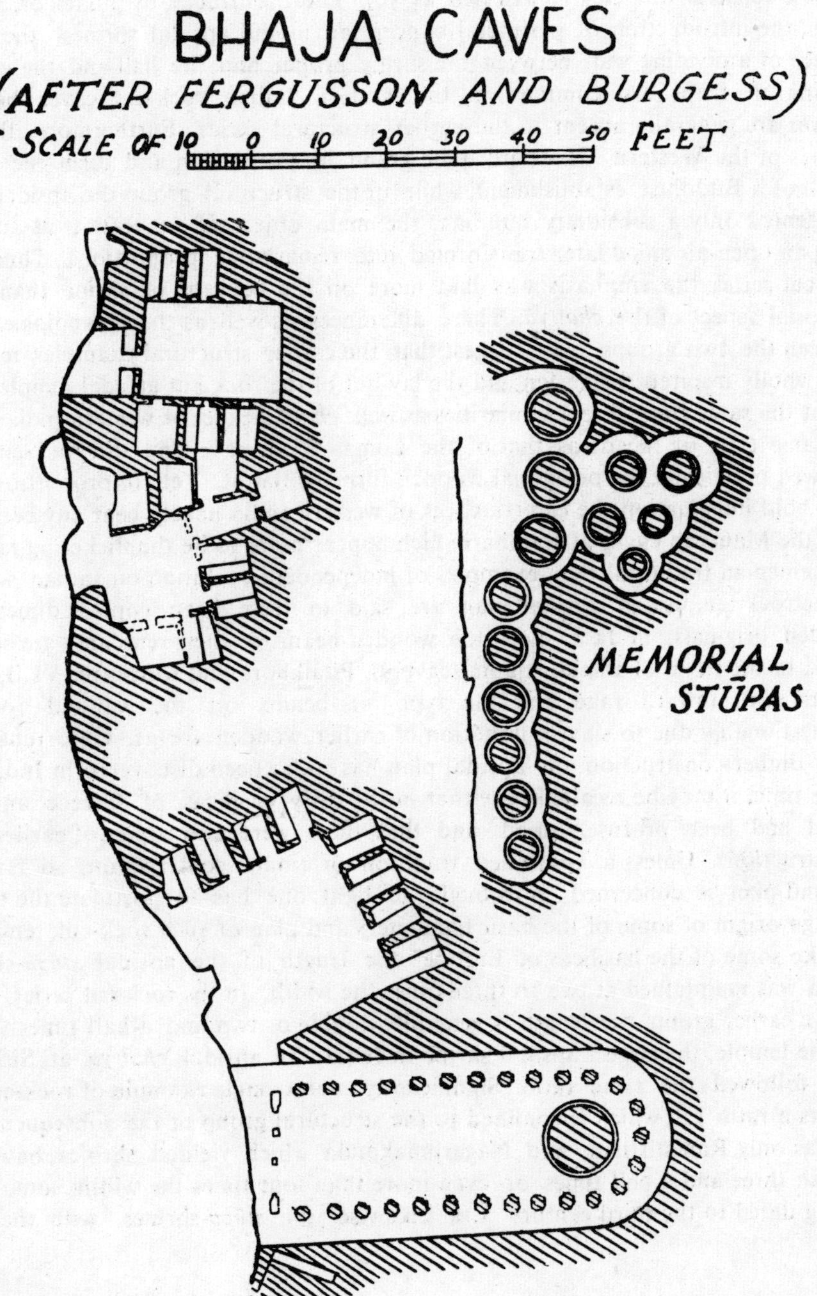
BHAJA CAVES
(AFTER FERGUSSON AND BURGESS)
SCALE OF 10 0 10 20 30 40 50 FEET
MEMORIAL STŪPAS

FIG. 11

the west coast is not clearly assessed as yet. The occurrence of pillars or, in other words, the introduction of peripteral conception in the apsidal shrines, the general absence of a dividing-wall between the shrine proper and the hall and the entrance-opening in front are common in the western Indian rock-cut caves but these features are generally absent in the earlier structural series. Furthermore, the cave-temples of the Western Ghats are quite grand in proportion and form the primary edifice of a Buddhist establishment, while in the structural group the apsidal shrines represented only a subsidiary building, the main object of veneration at such sites being an open-air *stūpa* later transformed into remarkable proportions. Thus, in the rock-cut series the emphasis was laid more on the concept of shrine than on the memorial aspect of the *chaitya*. These differences as well as the chronological hiatus between the two groups may suggest that the earlier structural examples might not have wholly inspired the design and the lay-out of the rock-cut apsidal temples. There are, at the same time, a few similarities as well: *chaitya*-caves of western India adopted the same type of façade as that of the Lomas Rishi cave and the rock-cut pillars followed practically the octagonal wooden form of Bairat. Yet, in proportion as well as in bold imagination the *chaitya*-caves of western India hardly bear any comparison with the Mauryan caves at Barabar which appear more to be the flickering rays of an Achaemenian tradition[1] than examples of independent evolution on Indian soil.

The rock temples of apsidal plan are said to have been copied directly from wooden originals; in fact, even the wooden beams or their remnants are still to be found in the caves of Bhaja, Ajanta (cave 9), Pitalkhora and Karle (pl. VI B; fig. 12). Pillars with inward rake and the type of beams on the vaulted roof were unquestionably due to slavish imitation of earlier wooden forms. Unfortunately, no such timber-construction on apsidal plan has so far been discovered in India; at the same time, it may be recalled here that in the early basilicas of Greece and Rome wood had been profusely used, and that these were also copies of earlier timber-constructions. Unless a continued tradition of timber-construction, so far as this ground-plan is concerned, is brought to light one has to postulate the theory of foreign origin of some of the basic characters and plan of such rock-cut temples.

Like some of the basilicas of Europe[2] the length of the apsidal *stūpa*-shrines in India was maintained at two to three times the width. In the rock-cut series, specially in the earlier group, the length is generally double or two and a half times the width of the temple; the largest apsidal shrine in India, the apsidal *chaitya* at Sirkap (fig. 13), followed the same ratio. Significantly, not a single example of rock-cut shrine shows a ratio 1:3, which is confined to the structural group of the subsequent period. It was only Ramatirtham and Nagarjunakonda which yielded shrines having their length three and a half times or even more than four times the width, some of them being dated to the third century A.D. Likewise, the *stūpa*-shrines, with their length

[1] Percy Brown, *Indian Architecture* (Buddhist and Hindu Periods), p. 24.

[2] Banister Fletcher, *op.cit.*, p. 201

TABLE I

A list of apsidal stūpa-shrines in India

Name of site	Length	Width	Type	Date	Reference
Bhaja	59′0″ 17·98 m	26′8″ 8·13 m.	rock-cut	2nd century B.C.	Fergusson and Burgess (1880), p. 224
Bedsa	45′4″ 13·82 m.	21′0″ 6·40 m.	,,	,,	,, p. 230
Kondane	66′6″ 20·27 m.	26′8″ 8·13 m.	,,	,,	,, p. 220
Ajanta, cave 9	45′0″ 13·72 m.	22′9″ 6·93 m.	,,	1st century B.C.	,, p. 290
Ajanta, cave 10	95′6″ 29·11 m.	41′1″ 12·52 m.	,,	2nd century B.C.	,, p. 293
Pitalkhora, cave 3	86′0″ 26·21 m.	35′0″ 10·67 m.	,,	,,	Deshpande (1959) p. 72
Pitalkhora, cave 10	17′7″ 5·36 m.	8′4″ 2·54 m.	,,	1st century B.C.—1st century A.D.	,, p. 78
Pitalkhora, cave 12	21′8″ 6·60 m.	7′6″ 2·29 m.	,,	1st century B.C.	,, p. 79
Pitalkhora, cave 13	27′10″ 8·48 m.	15′0″ 4·57 m.	,,	,,	,, p. 79
Kanheri	86′6″ 26·37 m.	39′10″ 12·14 m.	,,	2nd century A.D.	Fergusson and Burgess (1880) p. 352
Karle	124′3″ 37·87m.	45′6″ 13·87 m.	,,	1st century A.D.	,, pp. 233-34
Nasik	38′10″ 11·83 m.	21′7″ 6·58 m.	,,	,,	,, p. 274
Junnar	40′0″ 12·19 m.	21′7″ 6·58 m.	,,	,,	,, p. 254
Aurangabad	38′0″ 11·58 m.	22′8″ 6·91 m.	,,	2nd-3rd century A.D.	James Burgess (1878), p. 73
Junagarh	26′0″ 7·92 m.	20′0″ 6·10 m.	,,	,,	Fergusson and Burgess (1880), p. 195
Sana	31′0″ 9·45 m.	18′0″ 5·49 m.	,,	,,	,, p. 203
Karad	33′0″ 10·06 m.	12′0″ 3·66 m.	,,	,,	,, pl. V

Name of site	Length	Width	Type	Date	Reference
Ajanta, cave 19	46'0" 14·02 m.	24'0" 7·32 m.	rock-cut	5th century A.D.	Fergusson and Burgess (1880), p. 315
Ajanta, cave 26	67'10" 20·68 m.	36'3" 11·05 m.	,,	,,	,, p. 343
Ellora	85'10" 26·16 m.	43'0" 13·11 m.	,,	,,	,, p. 377
Dhamnar	23'6" 7·16 m.	15'0" 4·57 m.	,,	,,	p. 393
Sanchi, temple 40	67'0" 20·42 m.	22'0" 6·71 m.	Structural	3rd century B.C.	Marshall and Foucher
Sarnath	82'6" 25·14 m.	38'10" 11·83 m.	,,	,,	*An. Rep. A.S.I.*, 1914, p. 100
Temple 13, Dharmarājikā	60'0" 18·29 m.	20'0" 6·10 m.	,,	1st century A.D.	Marshall (1951)
Sirkap	129'0" 39·32 m.	51'0" 15·54 m.	,,	1st century B.C.—1st century A.D.	,,
Kalawan	50'0" 15·24 m.	26'6" 8·08 m.	,,	1st century A.D.	,,
Nagarjunakonda Site 1	42'0" 12·80 m.	12'0" 3·66 m.	,,	3rd century A.D.	Sarkar (1960)
Nagarjunakonda Site 2	24'0" 7·32 m.	10'0" 3·05 m.	,,	,,	,,
Nagarjunakonda Site 3	26'0" 7·93 m.	11'0" 3·35 m.	,,	,,	,,
Nagarjunakonda Site 4	14'0" 4·27 m.	7'0" 2·13 m.	,,	,,	,,
Nagarjunakonda Site 5	36'0" 10·97 m.	12'0" 3·66 m.	,,	,,	,,
Nagarjunakonda Site 9	30'0" 9·14 m.	10'0" 3·05 m.	,,	,,	,,
Nagarjunakonda Site 23	26'0" 7·93 m.	8'0" 2·44 m.	,,	,,	,,
Nagarjunakonda Site 26	30'0" 9·14 m.	11'0" 3·35 m.	,,	,,	,,
Nagarjunakonda Site 32	14'0" 4·27 m.	8'0" 2·44 m.	,,	,,	,,

Name of site	Length	Width	Type	Date	Reference
Nagarjunakonda Site 43	32′0″ 9·75 m.	11′0″ 3·35 m.	Structural	3rd century A.D.	Sarkar (1960)
Nagarjunakonda Site 51	18′0″ 5·49 m	7′0″ 2·13 m.	,,	,,	,,
Nagarjunakonda Site 106	17′0″ 5·18 m.	7′0″ 2·13 m.	,,	,,	,,
Nagarjunakonda Site 108	27′0″ 8·23 m.	11′0″ 3·35 m.	,,	,,	,,
Ramatirtham-1	40′0″ 12·19 m.	11′0″ 3·35 m,	,,	—	*An. Rep. A.S.I.* 1910-11
,, -2	26′9″ 8·15 m.	11′0″ 3·35 m.	,,	—	,,
,, -4	33′5″ 10·18 m.	11′6″ 3·50 m.	,,	—	,,
,, (Durgakonda)	60′0″ 18·29 m.	13′0″ 3·96 m.	,,	—	,,
,, -5	30′0″ 9·14 m.	13′6″ 4·11 m.	,,	—	,,
Sankaram	44′5″ 13·54 m.	29′7″ 9·02 m.	,,	—	,,
,,	21′0″ 6·40 m.	15′0″ 4·57 m.	,,	—	,,
Udayagiri	78′1″ 23·80 m.	21′8″ 6·60 m.	,,	—	*Indian Archaeology 1958-59—A Review*, pp. 38-40
Brahmagiri	23′0″ 7·01 m.	13′0″ 3·96 m.	,,	—	*Ancient India no. 4* (1948), p. 186

one and a half times the width, made their emergence only between the third and fifth centuries A.D.

To establish the relationship of one group with the other on the basis of the common ratio between the length and the width is no doubt difficult but the evidence is suggestive of some common link existing between the two geographically-separated series of apsidal buildings. One may assume that this form evolved in India out of elliptical or circular plans of the Barabar group of caves by way of combining the separate cella with the oblong antechamber or by dividing the elliptical halls into two halves, like the ones at Rajgir (above, p. 17), into apsidal outline. In support of the former hypothesis one may cite the example of cave 13 at Pitalkhora (fig. 9), with

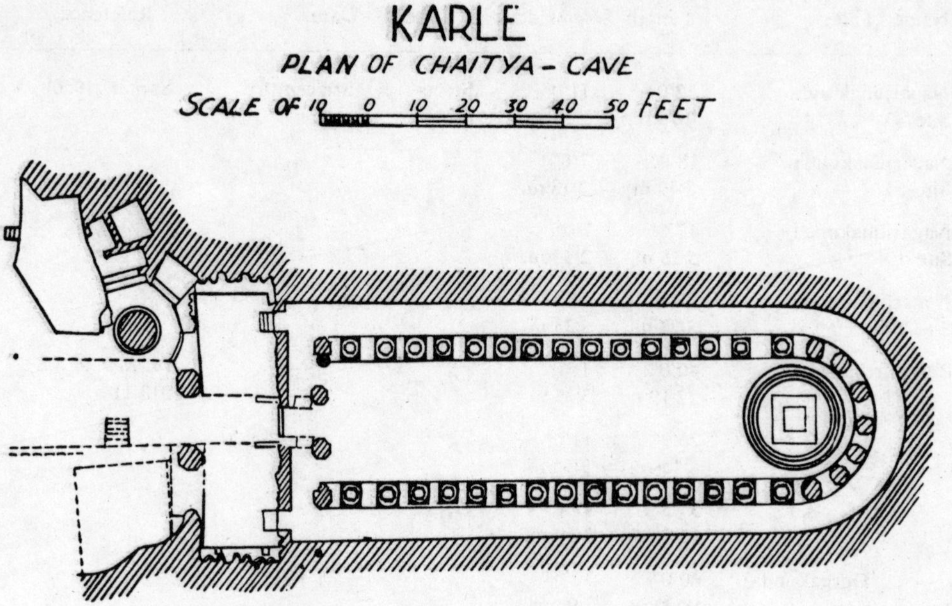

FIG. 12

a clearly circular end; supporting evidence in favour of the second alternative is not available as yet. It does not necessarily exclude the possibility of the elliptical structures of Rajgir being remotely connected in some way or the other with the rise of the apsidal buildings in India inasmuch as the Buddhist might not have acceded to the importing of an alien form had not an earlier tradition resembling the apsidal outline persisted in the country. Further, the apsidal form may easily be considered as an imitation of the sacred *Buddhapāda*,[1] so common in the artistic representations of the early periods.

All the above-mentioned alternatives are mere theoretical considerations and, truly speaking, no plan or basic characters of a religious edifice can evolve without any direct relation to civil architecture of a country. The apsidal plan was absolutely foreign to India, and for its introduction certain impetus from outside seems to be a necessary precondition. Percy Brown[2] has already pointed out that 'the most striking fact in connection with the plan and general design of the Buddhist Chaitya hall is its undeniable resemblance to the Graeco-Roman basilica, a type of structure which was being evolved in Europe about the same time'. But he adds that, 'In spite of this similarity and their almost contemporaneous emergence it is extremely unlikely that the two forms of hall were in any way related'. He thus assumes the theory of an independent evolution of apsidal shrines in India from a 'primitive beginning'.

[1] This was suggested by Shri B. M. Pande of Archaeological Survey of India.
[2] Percy Brown, *op. cit.*, p. 25.

which really speaking, is difficult to reconstruct : neither its true timber-prototypes nor the apsidal ground plan, not to speak of rock-architecture, existed in India. On the contrary, apsidal structures were certainly in vogue in Palestine,[1] Crete and Greece[2] prior to their emergence in India. When this plan was so widely used in several countries outside India, the origin and history of such structures will have to be viewed in a wider perspective, for India was not a closed door all through her history.[3]

The early concentration of rock-cut apsidal shrines on the west coast, the area of continued foreign contact, might not have been a sheer accident because this region felt the impact of foreign ideas even from the time of Aśoka when a *Yavana* king Tushāspha adorned the lake Sudarśana with conduits.[4] Also there exists a tradition that Moggaliputta Tissa selected for missionary work Elder, Dharmarakshita, who was sent to Aparāntaka (Chapter VI). Over and above, inscriptions[5] from Karle, Junnar and Nasik clearly reveal that the *Yavanas*, Śakas, etc. participated in the construction of these cave-temples. At least fourteen donors of the *chaitya*-cave at Karle hailed from Dhenukākaṭa, out of which about five were *Yavanas*; evidently, it denotes the presence of a *Yavana* colony in that place. Again, the majority of the gifts came from the merchant communities living at important centres of trade like Surpāraka or Sopara, Nasik, Paiṭhān, Kalyāṇa, Dhenukākaṭa,[6] Vanavāsī etc. These traders and merchants were not only the owners of the country's surplus wealth but were also carriers of new ideas and experiences that they might have encountered in distant lands. As an outcome of such contacts and, also because of the presence of the *Yavanas* and other foreign elements in western as well as in north-western India, the percolation of foreign ideas in respect of building or rock-architecture from different directions, consequently the emergence of new architectural forms by imbibing new ideas, was more a natural process than anything otherwise.

It is interesting to note that the apsidal *stūpa*-shrines did not find much favour with the Buddhist sects of north India as their occurrence there compared to that of the coastal region was only few and far between. It is also uncertain whether this type of *stūpa*-shrine continued even after the early Christian era, specially after the introduction of Buddha image; one example datable to the second-fourth century A.D. is reported from Kumrahar[7] but the identification leaves much room for doubt.

[1] W. F. Albright, *The Archaeology of Palestine* (Penguin books, 1960), pp. 70-72.

[2] A. W. Lawrence, *Greek Architecture* (Pelican History of Art, 1957), pp. 53-54.

[3] 'Lydian excavated and monolithic tombs at Pinara and Xanthos on the south coast of Asia Minor present some analogy with the early Indian rock-cut caitya halls.' See Ananda K. Commaraswamy, *History of Indian and Indonesian Art* (London, 1927), p. 12.

[4] *Epigraphia Indica,* VIII, pp. 36 ff.

[5] J. Burgess, *Report on the Buddhist Cave Temples and their inscriptions,* Archaeological Survey of Western India, IV (London, 1883), pp. 82-116; also see Lüders' list, *Epigraphia Indica,* X.

[6] The place is not yet properly identified, but this locality appears to be in western India.

[7] A. S. Altekar and Vijayakanta Mishra, *Report on Kumrahar Excavations 1951-55* (Patna, 1959), p. 57, pl. XXXI. Another structure from the same site (p. 38, pl. XIII) has been identified as an apsidal *chaitya*, datable to the second century B.C. to first century A.D., but it is also a doubtful case.

Harwan[1] in Kashmir, however, disclosed an apsidal *stūpa*-shrine ascribable to the fourth century A.D.; this was built on the analogy of the Taxila group of shrines. Temple 18 of Sanchi datable to the seventh century appears to be one of the latest examples of *stūpa*-chapel; here columns were used like those of the western Indian cave-temples.

In order to make the present study a comprehensive one it is felt necessary to state here a few salient features of the apsidal *stūpa*-chapels at Taxila and of the east coast. From the point of view of structural plan the *griha-stūpas* of Taxila (also below, pp. 50 ff.) revealed two major types, viz., (i) apsidal and its cognate form and (ii) quadrangular, the latter variety being the most popular there, is dealt in the next section. Sirkap specimen[2] (fig 13), the largest in India and the earliest not only in Taxila but also

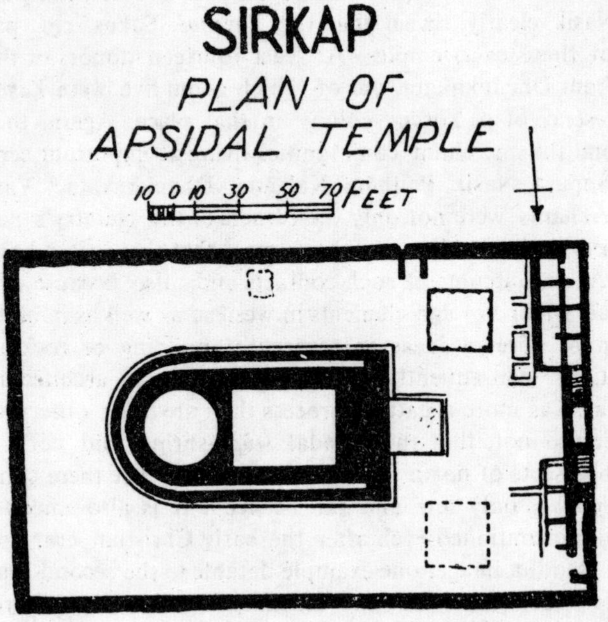

FIG. 13

in north-west India, had its apse differentiated from the nave by a screen. Similarly, the columns had also been wholly dispensed with. Typologically Taxila ones were thus related more to the Barabar caves or the Mauryan apsidal temples than with

[1] Ramachandra Kak, *op. cit.*, pp. 108-11.

[2] Marshall (1951), *op cit.*, p. 151. A circular brick wall, with a probable diameter of 208 ft., from Lauriya Nandangarh was thought by N. G. Majumdar to be a part of an apse of an apsidal temple (*Annual Report of Arch. Surv. of Ind., 1935-36*, p 63). In the absence of proper drawing or photograph it is difficult to verify the suggestion put forth by Majumdar. The structure was dated to the second century B.C.

the western Indian series. A unique contribution of Taxila to the development fo apsidal shrine was the use of octagonal apse: in case of I 3 of the Dharmarājikā (fig. 9) the interior of the apse was octagonal whereas A 1 of Kalwan (fig. 9) consisted of an octagonal shrine with antechamber in front. These are only isolated trends which perhaps entered into this country in the trail of intensive foreign contact. Yet in Taxila the *stūpa*-shrines had never been allowed to overshadow the main *chaitya*. Further, such apsidal shrines, notwithstanding their early occurrence, failed to receive any patronage from the Buddhist sects residing in the Taxila region, and the history of the apsidal temples there comprised only about half a century. It may tend to show that such buildings had no roots in the soil and the grafted tradition there withered away like that of the Ganga plane in no time.

No apsidal *stūpa*-shrine seemed to have been constructed in Taxila after the first century A.D. But the east coast of India during the early Christian era saw a brisk structural activity producing a number of apsidal buildings, the majority of which fall in the third century A.D. Not much information in respect of the evolution of the apsidal shrines in western India comes after the second century A.D. Most probably the shifting of the Sātavāhana capital to Dharanikota near Amaravati, Andhra Pradesh, in the lower Krishna basin drew a curtain for the time being on the intensive architectural activities that produced a rich harvest of cave-temples on the western sea-board. For subsequent development of this form one must, therefore, turn to the east coast which soon emerged as the cultural epicentre of the entire Deccan plateau under the patronage of the later Sātavāhans, and then under the Ikshvāku rulers. As already stated (p. 30) practically all the apsidal temples of this coastal tract were made of bricks yet the greatest change that ushered in was the transformation of apsidal temples into image-shrines some time in the last quarter of the third century A. D. A clear picture of this change came from Nagarjunakonda which laid bare about a score of apsidal shrines meant either for the *stūpa* or for the image of Buddha.

For the development of apsidal *chaitya-gṛihas* on the east coast one has to make a survey of four sites, viz., (i) Udayagiri, (ii) Ramatirtham, (iii) Sankaram and (iv) Nagarjunakoda. Of these, the apsidal *stūpa*-shrine at Udayagiri[1], District Puri, Orissa, appears to be the earliest; it has, however, been identified as a Jain temple. No less than six examples were unearthed at Ramatirtham[2] in Visakhapatnam District of Andhra Pradesh. There were two *chaitya-gṛihas*, nos. 1 and 4 of Rea's plan, with their length three and a half times the width—the one from the adjoining Durgakonda having its length more than four and a half times the width. In such cases of narrow breadth circumabulation must not have been possible: at Nagarjunakonda there was practically no space between the *stūpa* and the wall of the apse in the majority of the examples. Besides, this practice of circumabulation was perhaps considered unnecessary because of the existence of a principal *stūpa* at the site. Again, the presence of screen-wall between the shrine and the antechamber also made circumabulation a

1 *Indian Archaeology 1958-59—A Review*, pp. 30-40.
2 *Annual Report of the Archaeological Survey of India, 1910-1911*, pl. XL.

difficult task. Such a screen-wall existed in chaitya 1 at Ramatirtham though it was absent practically in all the *stūpa*-shrines of the east coast; Nagarjunakonda too did not reveal this feature which was confined there only to the apsidal image-shrines, Further, none of the *chaitya gṛihas* at Nagarjunakonda (pl. XIII), Ramatirtham and Sankaram[1] yielded columns so conspicuous in the western Indian caves; an apsidal Śiva shrine from Nagarjunakonda, however, had pillars along the apsidal outline of the structure. Mention may be made here of the fact that caves 10 and 12 of Pitalkhora,[2] and an apsidal temple at Karad[3] were designed without pillars: the Bawā Pyārās Math at Junagarh,[4] however, had only four pillars. Whether this design was due to some misconception that columns had no utility from the point of view of stability of structures or was modelled after some other building tradition like the one of the Barabar caves is not clear. Nevertheless, the structural examples with a few exceptions entirely dispensed with the columns because they were found unnecssary from the point of view of stability, and in addition to that, the narrow width did not also permit so many pillars to crowd inside the hall.

The Buddhist architecture on the east coast thus combined in its texture two traditions—the early tradition of raising of *stūpas* and the conception of *chaitya-gṛiha*. This synthesis had its beginning at Taxila but it was Nagarjunakonda which harmonized the two different traditions into a balanced architectural plan. The idea of transforming apsidal *stūpa*-chapel into on image-shrine possibly evolved at Nagarjunkonda, for there is hardly any image-shrine having an apsidal plan in western India. During third-fourth century A.D. square or oblong image-shrine also made its appearance at Nagarjunakonda – most likely this tradition too derived its origin from Taxila or Gandhāra. From the east coast the venue of Buddhist architectural movement shifted again to the western region, eventually resulting into an artistic efflorescence that has no parallel in the history of India. In this period Buddha figure appeared on the *stūpa*-faces of the apsidal shrines of Ajanta (pl. VII B) and Ellora although square or oblong cella by then (fifth-sixth century A.D.) had attained greater popularity; above all, the image of Buddha had started replacing the *stūpa*, the aniconic symbol of the Master.

3. QUADRILATERAL

The *stūpas* in India were sometimes housed also inside the quadrilateral chapels, which in the passage of time superseded other types, for all the later Buddhist temples like Bodh-Gaya, Nalanda, Ajanta, Ellora etc. conform either to square or oblong plan. When exactly this form made its appearance in the domain of Buddhist architecture is difficult to say as the secular architecture of the protohistoric and ancient periods shows a clear predilection for this type of house-plan. In the archaeological

1 *An. Rep. Arch. Surv. Ind., 1908-09*, pp. 149-80.
2 M. N. Deshpande, *op. cit.*, pl. XLVI.
3 Fergusson and Burgess, *op. cit.*, pl. V.
4 *Ibid.*, pl. II.

records the cave-temples at Kuda appear to be the earliest remains of Buddhist quadrilateral *stūpa*-shrine though its period of emergence might not have been far removed in point of time from the *gṛiha-stūpa*, A 14, of the Kalawan monastery at Taxila, ascribable to the latter half of the first century A.D.

In spatial distribution this form embraces a rather restricted area, again with concentration on the west coast specially during the early Christian eras when a few oblong *gṛiha-stūpas* came up also at Taxila. The entire Ganga-Yamuna *doab* and the east coast seem to have been devoid of such monuments; this form, however, had its later extension at Bagh[1] and Dhamnar[2], both being in central India. But its occurrence at Kuda, Mahad, Karad[3], Sailarwadi, Junnar, Kanheri etc.[4] clearly suggests western India as the focal point of this type of *stūpa*-shrines.

These quadrilateral rock-cut chapels (fig. 14) are mostly without pillars, their dimensions being comparatively smaller the necessity for providing columns was not possibly felt at all. At Kuda the caves comprised a cella and a vestibule, the latter built on pillars varying in number from two to four. In majority of the cases the back wall of the *stūpa*-shrine was cut longer than the front one although at Mahad and Karad the sides are more or less equal In all the cases the vestibule is differentiated from the shrine proper like that of the apsidal chapels of Taxila: even the *gṛiha-stūpa* of Kalawan[5] monastery had an oblong cella separated from the antechamber. Yet the Taxila group taken as a whole differs from the western Indian series in having quadrangular *stūpa*-shrines within the monastic enclosures; such shrines came from Chir Topes B and C, and possibly at Mohra Moradu but each of these establishments had its principal *stūpa* as well (Chapter IV). Unlike Taxila the monastic establishments at Kuda, Mahad, Karad etc., showed emphasis exclusively on the *chaitya*-shrines—the Bagh and Dhamnar caves inheriting an identical conception probably from western India. But so far as the constructional aspects are concerned the Taxila group bears certain similarity with the western Indian quadrilateral *stūpa*-shrines despite the fact that both the regions were separated geographically. Whether both the traditions derived their forms from one common source or the region influenced the other can not be determined without further research and discovery in the archaeological field. Further, why this type did not spread to the east coast is also not easily explainable. Obviously this form did not appeal much to the Buddhists until this very ground-plan was adopted for enshrining the image of Buddha practically in all parts of India.

Now, wherefrom did the Buddhists derive this architectural conception? No archaeological evidence of temples of this form prior to the Gupta period is as yet known; the earliest remains of a Brahmaṇical structure are, however, the foundations

[1] John Marshall and others, *the Bagh Caves in the Gwalior State* (London, 1927).

[2] Fergusson and Burgess, *op. cit.*, pp. 393-95.

[3] Jas Burgess, *Report on the Buddhist Cave temples and their inscriptions*, Archaeological Survey of western India, IV (London, 1883), pls. VIII-X for Kuda, Mahad and Karad.

[4] Fergusson and Burgess, *op. cit.*, pls. V, XVIII and LIII for Sailarwadi, Junnar and Kanheri.

[5] Marshail (1951), pl, 326 ff.

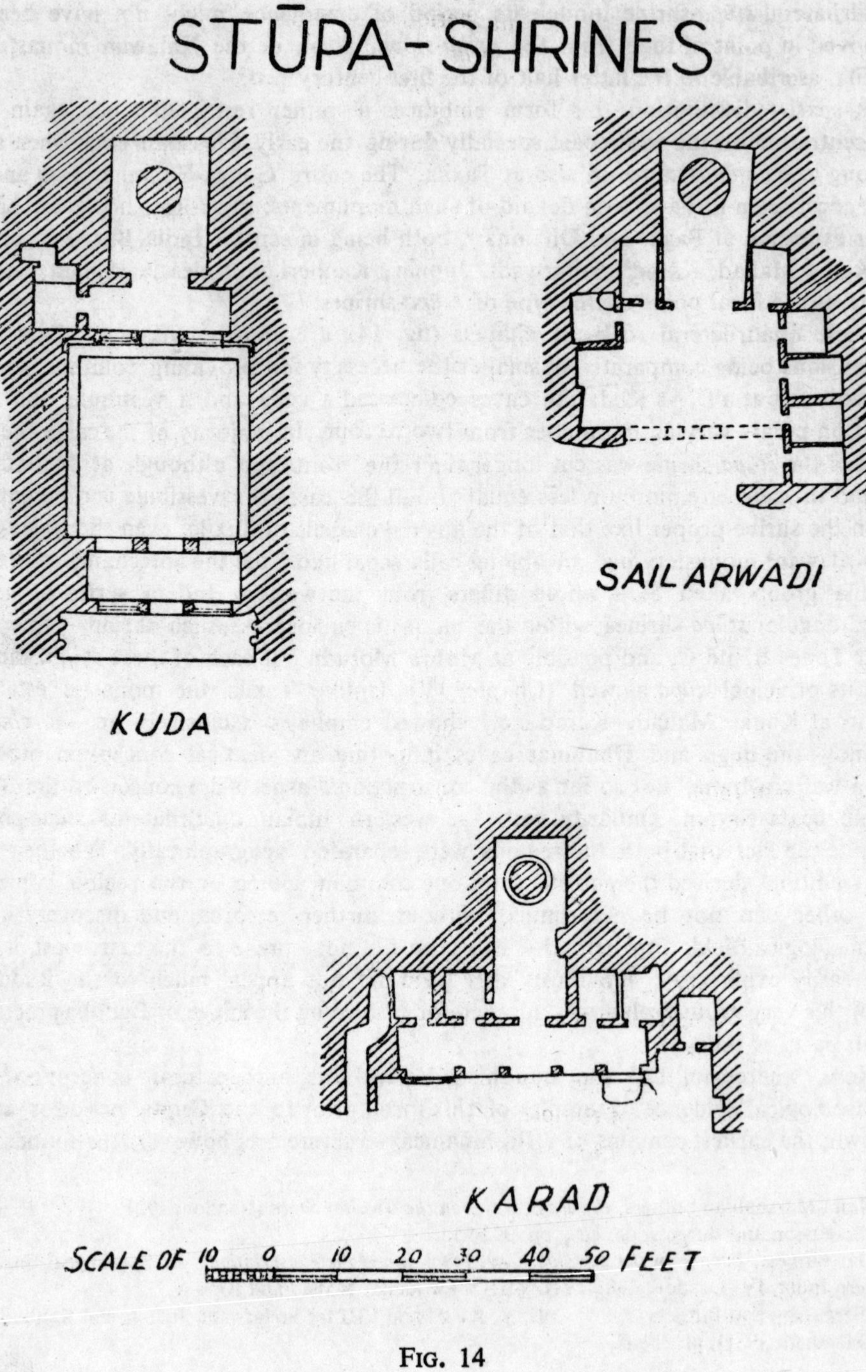
STŪPA-SHRINES
SAILARWADI
KUDA
KARAD
SCALE OF 10 0 10 20 30 40 50 FEET

FIG. 14

of a Vishṇu temple at Besnagar discovered in close proximity to the Heliodoros pillar.[1] The temple is generally dated to the second century B.C.; it had possibly an elliptical (above, p. 22) ground-plan. At the same time one cannot wholly discount the possibility of a square or rectangular shrines being evolved independently in India out her own building tradition but a doubt creeps in once the early distribution of quadrilateral *stūpa*-shrines in the west coast and in the Taxila region is taken into account, for both these regions felt the impact of foreign inroads, ideologically and politically, to a maximum extent. In the circumstances, the infiltration of certain extraneous building tradition in finally shaping the form of quadrangular *stūpa*-chapels appears to be reasonable hypothesis in the present state of archaeological investigation.

4. AŚOKA'S CONTRIBUTION

Of the three types of Buddhist *stūpa*-chapels the circular and the apsidal forms appear to have been introduced in India almost contemporaneously, and their time of emergence synchronized almost with the appearance of the monumental form of *stūpa* and importation of rock-cut architecture. As stated earlier (above, p. 4) the *stūpas* or *chaityas* either in the shape of a tumulus or made of perishable materials must have been in existence in India before Aśoka but undoubtedly this Maurya emperor was the first to impart architectural quality and a spirit of permanency to these memorials; his Nigali Sagar pillar-inscription dated in the fourteenth regnal year states the event of doubling the existing *stūpa* of Kanakamuni. How this idea of constructing or enlarging the *stūpa* dawned on his mind is not known; the traditional account that he constructed eightyfour thousand *stūpas* throughout the length and breadth of his empire would only reveal a conscious and determined effort on Aśoka's part to impose on his subjects, irrespective of their religious inclination, an architectural composition of much durable design. It was, however, only a facet of a multi-pronged movement which aimed, at least outwardly, at a lofty ideal of disseminating the teachings of Buddha through a number of tangible media like rock-edicts and other awe-inspiring monuments. Yet all these forms and contents were determined by his personal experience, taste and preference;[2] in other words, all his monuments as well as the art-forms did not always take into cognizance the collective outlook of his people, their preference, religious beliefs and practices.

For attaining his ideals Aśoka borrowed many architectural designs and structural plans from beyond the borders of Indian frontiers. The Achaemenian tradition made a deep impact on the selection of types and ornamentation of his pillars, pillar-capitals, rock-cut caves and stone-edicts.[3] In fact, India's dyke of isolation was breached earlier at the time of the Achaemenid occupation and the plantation

1 Percy Brown, *op. cit.*, 1957-58. For reference to early Vaishṇava shrines see, J.N. Banerjea. *The Development of Hindu Iconography*, (Calcutta, 1956), pp. 90-95.

2 Nihar Ranjan Ray, *Maurya and Suṅga Art* (Calcutta, 1945), p. 63.

3 *Ibid* pp. 31-32.

of Greek colonies like Nysa and the kingdom of Sophytes[1] on the north-west frontiers. These were followed by Alexander's invasion and the establishment of Greek kingdoms on Indian borders, thereby bringing India much nearer to Greece and the Mediterranean world. Indeed, the clash between Chandragputa and Seleukos Nicator proved to be an important landmark — a happy augury in the establishment of cultural contact between the two civilizations. Much new ideas, architectural forms and equipments of material culture trickled down through the crevices of mutual intercourse, with the result that the tide of change rippled past through many a realm of Indian culture and ideology.

In a stream of diverse foreign ideas it is not easy to recognize the particular wave of inspiration and its source. The Achaemenian traits in the Maurya art and architecture are more or less discernible but Greek contribution to their development requires a re-assessment. There were, in fact, two aspects of the Mauryan architectural achievements — permanent and short-lived; the latter comprised Aśokan edicts, cave-architecture and the Mauryan art, while the former included monumental form of *stūpa* and the concept of shrine and worship in Buddhist ideology. The evanescent aspect derived primarily from the Achaemenian culture did not last long after the collapse of the Mauryan empire. Despite the continuity of idea of shrine the architectural trends associated with circular or apsidal temples had also an uneven growth in India, specially the circular form of Buddhist shrines remained all along an inassimilable trait in an Indian setting.

Of the permanent contribution to Indian tradition the monumental form of the *stūpa* or *chaitya* ranks foremost in the list, with a long chain of subsequent evolution in India and abroad. Some authorities, however, postulate the existence of pre-Aśokan brick *stūpa* at Piprahwa on the basis of a reliquary inscription which has been interpreted differently by different scholars. Whatever may be the palaeographic date[2] of this find, architecturally the *stūpa* there in its present form, with a huge diameter of 116 ft. (35·36 m.), constructions in the form of concentric circles of brick and a circular well in the centre[3] can hardly claim such a high antiquity as the fourth-third century B.C.; in diameter it is almost as big as Sanchi and bigger than any *stūpa* at Nagarjunakonda or Sarnath. It seems, therefore, quite probable that no brick-built Buddhist *stūpa* prior to Aśoka was constructed in India although the tradition of earthen tumulus must have had a very long past.

To evolve an architectural form out of tumulus was not, of course, improbable, yet the idea to transform it into a lasting design surely anticipates a new vision, which was infused to it perhaps by Aśoka. It is not unlikely that the permanent form of the *tūpa* in India drew its inspiration, at least to a certain extent, from the brick-built tholos,[4] also memorial in character, of the Mediterranean countries.

1 H. C. Raychaudhuri, *Political History of Ancient India* (Calcutta, 1950), pp. 246-52.

2 For reference to different publications see D.C. Sircar, *op. cit.*, p. 84.

3 William Claxton Peppe, 'The Piprahwa Stūpa containing relics of Buddha', and 'Notes' by V. A. Smith, *The Journal of the Royal Asiatic Society of Great Britain and Ireland for 1958*, pp. 573-88.

4 A. W. Lawrence, *op. cit.*,pp. 57-64.

The simultaneous appearance of structural *stūpa* and the circular peripteral temple during the rule of Aśoka precludes the possibility of an independent evolution of the latter either from *stūpa* or from primitive circular huts. Moreover, the two groups of structural form represent two different concepts: the idea of worship appears to have been latent in the concept of shrine which was indeed incompatible with the original idea of *stūpa* representing a memorial. Thus the cult of *stūpa* during Aśoka's time itself was viewed from two different points of view—*stūpa* as an object of worship and as a memorial. As there was no time-gap between the two sets of idea the development of one from the other is difficult to formulate in the present state of archaeological research. Architecturally, the Bairat temple was unique in plan and also, as indicated above (p. 27), unique in conception; to think it, therefore, an Aśokan importation from outside India, probably from west Asia or from the Mediterranean countries, is not entirely without a basis. Aśoka maintained friendly relations with Antiochos II Theos, king of Syria and western Asia. Ptolemy II Philadelphos, king of Egypt, Magas, king of Cyrene in north Africa, Antigonos Gonatas, king of Macedonia and Alexander ruling over Epirus; his envoys, as he himself records it in Edict XIII, penetrated into these countries and he was also responsble for many philanthropic activities in their dominions. In such a state of intimate contact between India and other countries travelling of ideas and architectural designs was only a normal phenomenon.

That the concept of worship amongst the Buddhist developed to a great extent is amply borne out by the plastic representations of scenes of worship on the railings of Bharhut, Sanchi and Bodh-Gaya, all of them being ascribable to the Śuṅga period. So far as the present knowledge goes this idea of worship crept into the Buddhist fold during Aśoka's period: the differentiation of the shrine proper from the place of assembly in the Barabar caves also substantiates the hypothesis. This new practice grew into proportions and eventually put into shade the memorial aspect of the *stūpa*-cult, specially with the acceptance of the Buddha image by different Buddhist sects. On the contrary, the circular shrines failed to attain any popularity but for its sporadic occurrence. This lack of popular support for this type of architectural composition only brings out its imposed, at the same time, impermeable character.

The movement that produced the circular temple was also possibly responsible for the emergence of apsidal *stūpa*-shrines which in all likelihood was also initiated by Aśoka in that period of intensive foreign contact;[1] like circular ones these *stūpa*-chapels too did not assume wide vogue in the Maurya period. Even in the succeeding epochs their number in northern India was only a few; obviously, this architectural form had to fight hard to endure on the Indian soil specially in northern India. It has already been shown (p. 34) that this very trend might not have climaxed into rock-cut architecture of western India, neither were the Taxila ones the dying echo of the

[1] Coomaraswamy (1927), *op. cit.*, p. 12 writes, 'The cylindrical stūpa with drum in two stages, as seen at Bedsā and in the Kusāna period is identical in form with a Phoenician tomb at Amrith (Marath) in North Syria.'

Mauryan tradition, for more than one impulse, maybe from different directions, made their presence felt at different times.

There were at least two areas of early concentration: the activities on the west coast started with the most durable material some time in the second century B.C., while the closing years of the Christian era saw the appearance of a similar form in rubble masonry at Taxila. Both the traditions appear to have owed their origin to two different sources; whereas the examples from Taxila being devoid of any pillar were far removed from the wooden prototype—if at all this group of structures had evolved out of timber construction—the western Indian cave-temples are basically pillared timber-construction executed through the medium of rock. The latter bears a close resemblance to the conception of early basilicas of Europe, the main characteristic of which might have spread to the west coast in the wake of India's trade-relation with the outside world. Besides commercial intercourse, this region, as the epigraphical data reveal, had several colonies of the *Yavanas* who might have been instrumental in imparting new architectural conceptions in Indian building tradition. Dhenukākaṭa appears to be the largest *Yavana* settlement in western India; as late as the third century A.D. there existed a *Yavana* kingdom at Sañjayapurī, the modern Sanjan, near Bombay.[1] Inscriptions from Sanchi mention a locality, Setapatha, indicating thereby the existence of a colony of *Yavanas* (*Setapathiyasa yonasa*);[2] its exact location, however, is not known. Further, the *Yavana* invasion in the Madhyamikā region culturally might not have been as short-lived as the military operation.

All these events must have culminated in commingling of ideas, architectural conceptions and artistic visions ultimately giving birth to the social and artistic awakening of the Śuṅga and Sātavāhana periods. Art and architecture of these ages flourished not only on this cultural fusion, but also on economic prosperity which must have been the outcome of intensive commerial activities.

5. RESUME

It is evident from the preceding chapters that the early Buddhist architectural tradition made use of four different ground-plans, viz., elliptical, circular, apsidal and quadrilateral. Of the four types, elliptical ground-plan appears to be the earliest and was in vogue in India perhaps even before the time of Buddha. It, however, did not continue for long as there is hardly any archaeological evidence to prove its continuity beyond the early Christian era, except sporadically in the Brahmanical tradition.

Equally old were the circular building plans but so far there is no evidence to show that the Buddhists adopted it before Aśoka. Moreover, the perpiteral conception imposed on a circular plan, the typical instance of which comes from Bairat, might have drawn its inspiration from Greece or west Asia. It was Aśoka who also

[1] D.C. Sircar, 'Nagarjunakonda Inscription of the time of Abhira Vasushena, year 30, *Epigraphia Indica*, XXXIV, p. 199.

[2] Marshall and others, *op. cit.*, pp. 308 and 348.

introduced the rock-cut architecture in India and possibly the idea of apsidal temple, the latter being connected inseparably with the concept of shrine.

But with the introduction of the concept of shrine several practices like the worship of *chaitya* or tree and the raising of memorial *stūpas*—both the practices being taken over by the Buddhists from popular Indian customs—gradually relegated into background. Likewise, the secular basis of many of the Buddhist structural forms were gradually forgotten.

It has to be borne in mind that the Aśokan tradition did not possibly cast any substantial influence on the rock-cut *chaitya*-architecture of the western seaboard. Like Gandhāra the western coast served as a veritable gate of foreign contact, and many extraneous trends, including the rock-cut apsidal temples, penetrated through these openings into the Buddhist realm of architecture and ideology.

Of the four types of building designs, the apsidal ones seem to have no moorings in India, and the plan along with the circular Buddhist temples were eventually superseded by quadrilateral chapels, which continue to be the most popular form in Indian religious architecture. Paradoxically, the quadrilateral ground-plan was the most popular in ancient and protohistoric India but during these periods the emphasis was laid more on oblong or rectangular form, the earliest remains of which came from several Harappan sites: on the other hand, square or intended-to-be square was of rare occurrence. It was this latter form which the Buddhists took over quite late, and that too, when some outside trend, not differing much from an existing Indian structural tradition, made its presence felt in Gandhāra and in the west coast.[1]

[1] For 'Site 27 of Nagarjunakonda' on page 29, lines 12 and 16, please read 'Site 24 of Nagarjunakonda'.

CHAPTER FOUR

TAXILA

Of innumerable Buddhist sites in the ancient Gandhāra (modern Rawalpindi District of West Panjab and North-Western Frontier Province, West Pakistan), Taxila is by far the most well-known and the only site where prolonged and extensive excavations unearthed several Buddhist establishments (fig. 15) ranging in date from the first century B.C. to about sixth-seventh century. But the history of Buddhism there is much older, for it was Aśoka who must have erected *stūpas* and other edifices at Taxila while implementing his programme for popularizing the message of Buddha. No trace of any building of Aśoka's time has yet been discovered save a few fragments of Mauryan pillar[1] and an Aramaic inscription of the same period. The name Dharmarājikā itself, that being the name of the main *stūpa* at Taxila, may also suggest Aśoka's association with the site,[2] and no wonder, the original *stūpa*, like the ones at Sanchi, Bodh-Gaya and Amaravati, might have been engulfed subsequently each by a larger one at the same site. Thus, so far as the visible evidence of the Buddhist structural remains of Taxila is concerned the history dates back from about the first century B.C., which is also chronologically the starting point of the present survey.

Here an attempt is made to trace the gradual development of the Buddhist monuments at Taxila, and concurrently, the probable doctrinal changes; evidently, it does not aim at defining the minute constructional and artistic aspects which have been discussed at length by Marshall in his monumental work, *Taxila* (Cambridge, 1951), which is also the primary source of all the data presented in this study.

1. LOCATION OF THE SETTLEMENTS

The excavations between the years 1913 and 1934 unearthed more than thirty monastic settlements (fig. 15), generally sheltered among the hills on the southern parts of the valley. From the point of view of geographical proximity these monuments, as described by Marshall, may be divided into following seven groups.

Group A (*Chir Tope group of monasteries*).—The most important establishment of this group, and also the largest in Taxila, was the Dharmarājikā stūpa (fig. 16), locally known as Chir Tope. It had at least four phases which are referred to in this chapter as Dharmarājikā I, II, III and IV respectively. Situated little to the south and south-east of the *stūpa* was a group of five monasteries termed by Marshall

1 Marshall, *op. cit.*, I (Structural Remains), p. 22.
2 *Ibid*, pp. 234-35.

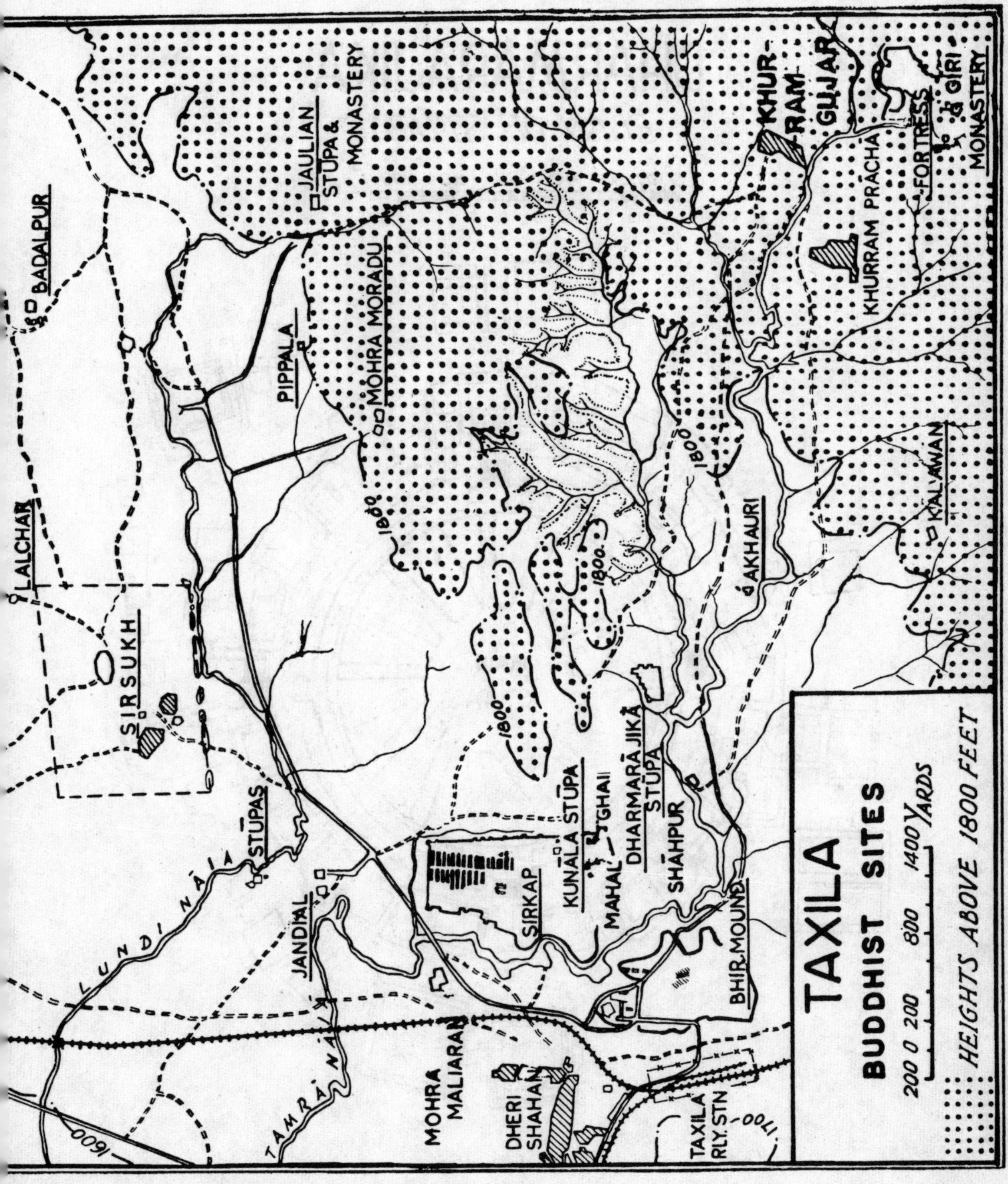
TAXILA
BUDDHIST SITES
200 0 200 800 1400 YARDS
HEIGHTS ABOVE 1800 FEET
LALCHAK
BADALPUR
JAULIAN STŪPA & MONASTERY
KHURRAM GUJAR
GIRI MONASTERY
FORTRESS
KHURRAM PRACHA
MOHRA MORADU
PIPPALA
SIRSUKH
STŪPAS
LUNDI NĀLA
JANDIAL
SIRKAP
KUNĀLA STŪPA
MAHAL
GHAI
DHARMARĀJIKĀ STŪPA
SHĀHPUR
BHIR MOUND
AKHAURI
KALAWAN
MOHRA MALIARAN
DHERI SHAHAN
TAMRĀ NĀLA
TAXILA RLY. STN
1800
1700
1600

FIG. 15

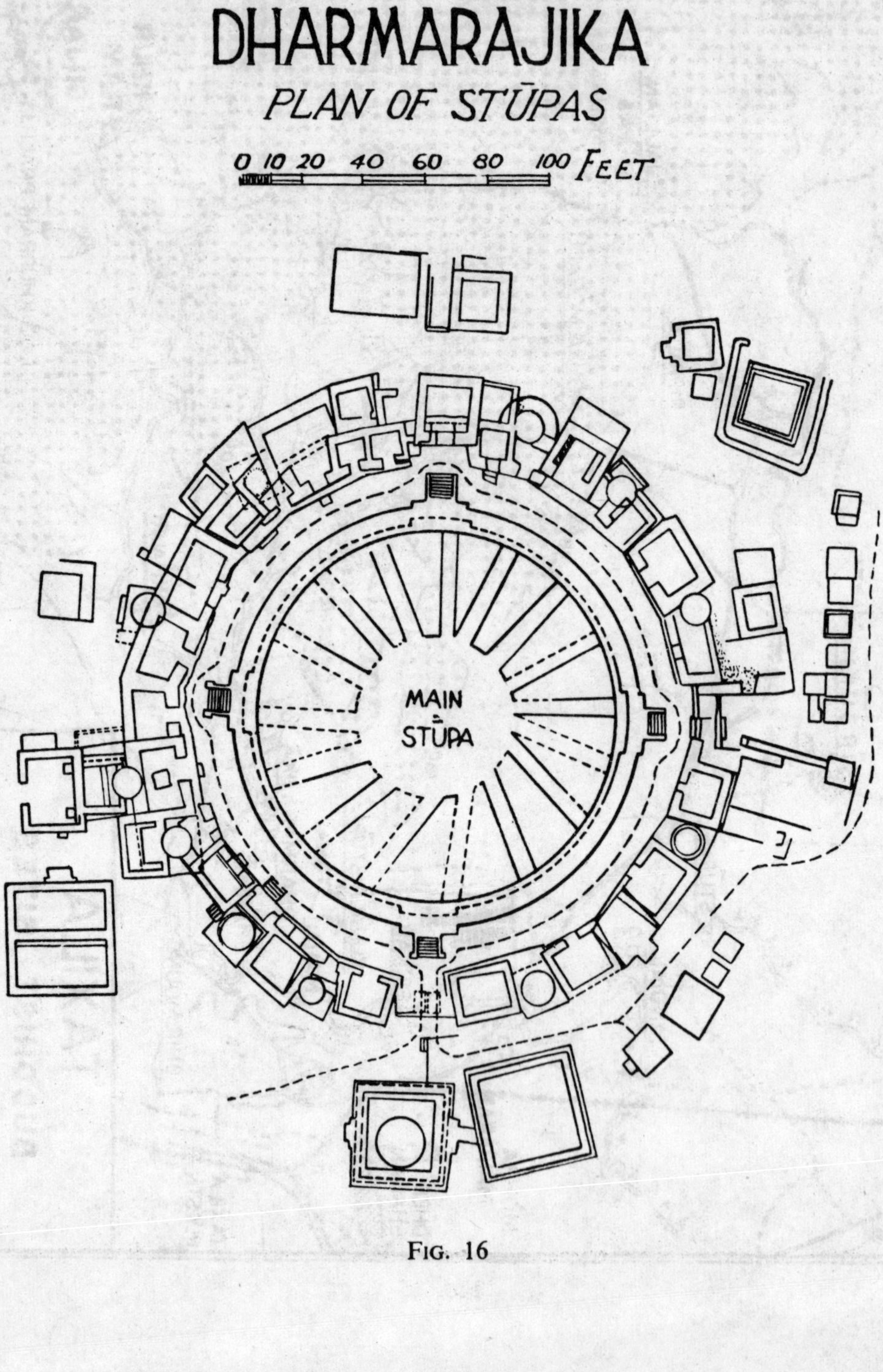
DHARMARAJIKA
PLAN OF STŪPAS
0 10 20 40 60 80 100 FEET
MAIN STŪPA

FIG. 16

as Chir Topes A, B, C, D1 and D2. The *stūpas* at Shahpur to the south of the Dharmarājikā had long disappeared; it appears, however, from Cunningham's report that the Stūpas 13 and 14 yielded inscriptions datable to the middle of the first century B.C.[1]

Group B (Kalawan group).—This was possibly an important centre of the Sarvāstivādin monks and gave rise to the second largest Buddhist foundation of Taxila. A smaller unit, Monastery H, situated near by, appears to have had no connexion with the main complex.

Group C (Giri).—Two self-contained units were laid bare in a secluded glen at Giri, about two miles to the east of Kalawan.

Group D (within the ancient limits of Sirkap).—There were at least two important establishments within the ancient limits of Sirkap, one of them named after Kuṇāla, the son of Aśoka, and the second one bore the name of the locality Gahi.[2] A third monastery to the south of Gahi was also located in a subsequent excavation.[3] All these remains are dated to the third or fourth century A.D., when Sirkap fell into ruins with the rise of Sirsukh, the third city of Taxila. Within the limits of Sirkap itself were unearthed *stūpas*, *gṛiha-stūpas* etc., the most imposing of them being an apsidal *stūpa*-chapel (fig. 13): no image-shrine seem to have been found. These were situated within the residential quarters and might not have been associated with any monastery.

Group E (around Sirkap).—Of this group the most important was the monastic site at Jandial having more than one phase. Cunningham's nos. 32 and 38½ were shrines situated at Mohra Maliaran but all their vestiges had long been razed to the ground.

Group F (around Sirsukh).—At a distance between two and three miles to the north-east of Sirkap but within an easy reach of Sirsukh once stood three *saṅghārāmas*, viz., Mohra Moradu (fig. 17), Pippala and Jaulian (fig. 18). Lalchak, an insignificant Buddhist settlement, was within two hundred yards from the north-east corner of Sirsukh; Badalpur,[4] however, would not be more than a mile to the west of the city.

Group G (isolated monastery).—The *stūpas* and monasteries at Bhamala (fig. 21) and Bhallar were far beyond the bounds of Taxila; in fact, the former was over nine miles from Sirsukh. On the testimony of Hiuen Tsang the Buddhist establishment at Bhallar[5] may possibly be ascribed to the Sautrāntika sect.

It is evident from the foregoing that with a few exceptions the different monasteries at Taxila grew around the main city. A glance at the map may show that the city of Taxila had a tendency to shift more and more towards the north-east, and the growth of monasteries there also followed almost a similar alignment. Without any

[1] Marshall, *op. cit.*, p. 7.

[2] Marshall spells it as 'Ghai', and Ghosh (see below) as 'Gahi'.

[3] A. Ghosh, 'Taxila (Sirkap), 1944-45', *Ancient India*, no 4 (1948), p. 44.

[4] *Archaeological Report North-western Frontier and Baluchistan* (1916-17), pp. 3-3. No detailed report on this site is available.

[5] Sir John Marshall, *A Guide to Taxila* (Cambridge, 1960), p. 178-79.

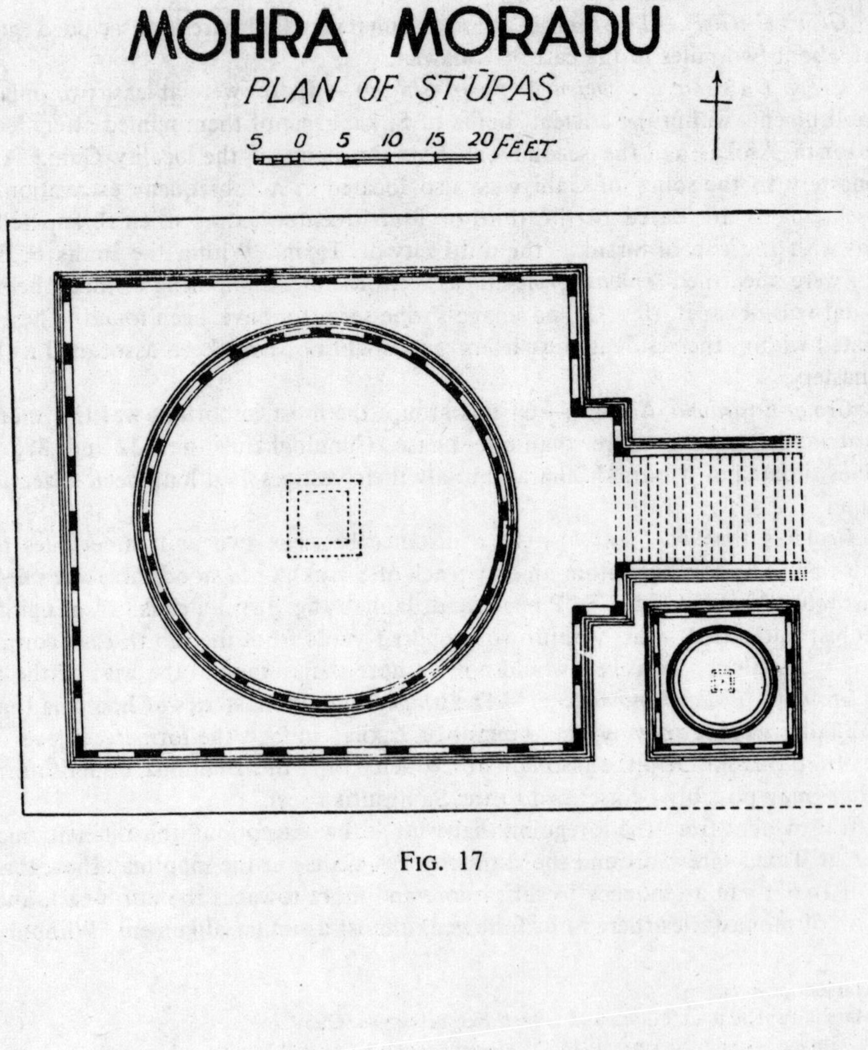

FIG. 17

doubt Groups E and F grew around Sirkap and Sirsukh respectively; also chronologically the latter group as a whole was posterior to the former one. Groups A and B were almost equidistant from Bhir Mound, the first city, and Sirkap, the second city. All these facts clearly demonstrate the dependence in some form or the other of the monastic habitations on the wealth and resources of Taxila; as a matter of fact, the surplus wealth of the city must have been diverted to a great extent towards the maintenance of a fairly large body of monks whose ideology in turn was exposed to the influence of being shaped and conditioned, at least to a certain degree, by traditional outlook and collective urge of the lay-community.

2. LAY-WORSHIPPERS AND THE BUDDHIST SAṄGHA

Besides the community of monks with their monasteries located outside the city, a large number of lay-worshippers, composed of heterogeneous elements, remained outside the pale of the Buddhist *saṅgha*. Of particular interest, therefore, was the discovery of more than half a dozen *stūpas* and *gṛiha-stūpas* situated within the residential quarters of Sirkap. Obviously, these were located in different parts of the city to enable the votaries to offer their worship in the shrines of their respective areas. On the other hand, extensively-excavated Nagarjunakonda did not produce such an evidence, where the monasteries were situated not far away from the habitational sites, yet there were only a few without a regular monastery to house the *saṅgha*. The general absence of independent shrines at Nagarjunakonda may tend to show that the laity had to offer their worship only at the monasteries occupied by a *saṅgha*, whereas at Sirkap the different groups of lay-worshippers had possibly had their own set of *stūpas* and *stūpa*-chapels.

How in such an early period as the first century A.D. the Buddhist religion could deviate so much from its original corporate ideals is difficult to find out. It is not unlikely that the Buddhist *saṅgha* might have been obliged to give such concession to the Saka-Parthians who not only held the political rein in that period but were also patrons of that religion. This individualistic concept in an extreme form might have reached Khotan where, as recorded by Fa-hien,[1] each family had a *stūpa* reared in front of the house.

The existence of private or public chapels does not necessarily mean that the lay-worshippers were apathetic towards the Buddhist church. Admittedly, no Buddhist *saṅgha* could have survived had not there been a large group of followers and lay-worshippers as their patrons whose gifts varied from the donation of a *stūpa*, *ārāma* etc., to the token gift of a small *stūpa*, or even a sculpture of Buddha. Broadly speaking, these gifts to the Buddhist *saṅgha* may be divided into two categories, viz., (i) gifts for the construction of the main edifices like *stūpa*, *ārāma* or *saṅghārāma*, and (ii) establishments of relics or *dhātu* and offerings in the shape of constructing miniature *stūpas*, image-chapels or donation of Buddha figures. Not many are the examples

[1] James Legge, *op. cit.*, p. 16.

from Taxila under the first category despite the fact that several early inscriptions[1] from Gandhāra and Mathurā regions allude to such type of gifts. The Taxila copper-plate inscription of a Meridarkh and the Taxila vase inscription discovered respectively from Cunningham's Stūpas 14 and 13 register the events of the construction of *stūpas* at Shahpur.[2] Such donations of *stūpas* or *saṅghārāma* depict a phase when the Buddhist establishments were being constructed for the acceptance of different Buddhist communities. Practically this phase represented the formative period in so far as the Buddhist structural movement was concerned; it had its beginning some time in the first century B.C. Not that no *vihāra* or *stūpa* was constructed after that date, but inscriptions do not make any mention to such gifts. This very omission may indicate that the Buddhist *saṅghas* in the beginning of their career there had to depend largely on the munificence of the foreign patrons, whereas in the succeeding epoch different sects could draw within their folds a large number of devotees who must have been at the beck and call of the Buddhist *saṅghas*.

Of the second category, the establishment of the corporeal relics had a long history dating back as early as the time of Menander,[3] and this practice might have survived in Gandhāra and in the neighbouring provinces even after the end of the first century A.D. On the other hand, the erection of image-chapels and the practice of offering Buddha image started from about the third quarter of the first century A.D.; the earliest known inscription recording the construction of *Bodhisattva-gṛiham* of Taxila is the silver scroll inscription (A.D. 79) discovered from G 5, an oblong shrine, to the north-west of the Dharmarājikā stūpa. Some of the inscribed images found in Building L to the south-west of the above-mentioned *stūpa* may easily be dated to the last quarter of the first century A.D. Even the practice of making gifts of Buddha images, which were often stored at Taxila in separate chapels, assumed wide vogue during Kanishka's rule (78-102 A.D.) not only in the Taxila region but also at Sarnath and Śrāvastī.[4] It is also certain from the inscriptions of Śrāvastī and Kalawan that the Sarvāstivādins took to image worship or, more precisely, allowed the laity to offer Buddha images, by about the end of the first century A.D.

The custom of raising miniature *stūpas* appears to be an older tradition than the offering of images or constructing image-chapels, because the ring of miniature *stūpas* around the Dharmarājikā came into existence during the first century B.C.

[1] For instance, the Mathura lion-capital inscriptions of the time of Rañjuvula (1-15 A.D.) and Soḍāsa (10-25 A.D), Mansehra inscription of the year 68, Peshawar Museum inscription no. 1, Kurram copper casket inscription (A.D. 99) of Kanishka, Khawat (Wardak) bronze vase inscription of Huvishka (129 A.D.) mention respectively of the gift of *stūpa* with *saṅghārāma*, an *ārāma*, a *stūpa* and *vihāra*. See Sten Konow, *Corpus Inscriptionum Indicarum*, II, i, pp. 30-49, 18-20, 127, 152 and 165.

[2] Sten Konow, *ibid.*, pp. 4-6.

[3] Shinkot steatite casket inscriptions of the time of Menander (*c.* 115-90 B.C) is one of the earliest Buddhist records of north-western India.

[4] Cf. Sārnāth Buddhist image-inscriptions (*Epigraphia Indica*, VIII, p. 173 ff.), Set-Mahet stone umbrella-staff (*ibid*, IX, p. 291) and Buddhist image inscriptions (*ibid*, VIII, p. 108 ff.) of the time of Kanishka.

Whether they were set up by the *saṅgha* itself or offered by the votaries from time to time is difficult to determine from meagre stratigraphical data; the former seems to be a possibility in view of the occurrence of array of *stūpas* or rows of chapels around the *mahā-chaityas* at several Gandhāra sites like Saha-ji-ki-dheri, Jamalgarhi, Takht-i-Bahi and so on. This characteristic feature of encircling the principal *stūpa* by subsidiary monuments was modelled possibly to substitute the railing so conspicuous in the early *stūpas* at Bharhut, Sanchi, Bodh-Gaya and Amaravati. It appears, therefore, that the Buddhist *saṅghas* might have given the lead in the introduction of miniature *stūpas*, which subsequently became an important item of gift by the lay-worshippers.

All the Buddhist sites at Taxila did not, however, yield miniature *stūpas*. For instance, Chir Topes A, C, D1 and D2, Kalawan (Monastery H), Giri A-B and Kuṇāla monastery were without this feature. It is apparent from Table II (p. 58) that the monastic establishments of Taxila may be divided into three groups from the point of view of the occurrence or absence of miniature *stūpas*. Group-A monasteries ranged in date from the first century A.D. to the third-fourth century A.D., while those under Group B from the first century A.D. to the fifth century. This division clearly shows the difference between the two groups; even the monasteries under Group C depict some attitude not wholly in conformity with those under Group B, where the laity had free scope to make meritorious gift for his spiritual attainment. The orthodox schools, possibly represented by Group-A monasteries, did not encourage the participation of the lay-worshippers in such activities. A similar principle appears to have been followed by the sects inhabiting the Group-C *saṅghārāmas*; the occurrence of a few examples of subsidiary *stūpas* at each site only shows that they were probably reared by the *saṅgha* itself for some reason, and that their attitude towards the laity did not possibly differ basically from the authors of Group-A monasteries.

The main idea behind all these gifts was to worship Buddha or *stūpa*, the latter being his aniconic representation, and in return to such respectful offerings the householders expected the welfare of his kinsmen, increase in the power and longevity of the ruling monarch or dynasty and so on. There even existed the belief that such munificence would lead to *nirvāṇa*. Almost an identical conception prevailed amongst the donors of Nagarjunakonda (below, pp. 74 ff.), and the similarity in this aspect is so striking between the two geographically-separated areas that one cannot but postulate certain commonness amongst different Buddhist schools of thought in respect of their attitude towards the laity. And it is this commonness which might have been responsible for the presence of dormant Mahāyānic ideals amongst the Sarvāstivādins and the Mahāsāṅghikas[1] (below, p. 71).

It is evident from different donative records that the path to spiritual attainment was made much simpler for the householders who were no longer obliged to renounce the world or to traverse the road of strict monastic rules of discipline. This relaxation

[1] Nalinaksha Dutt, *Aspects of Mahāyāna Buddhism and its relation to Hīnayāna* (London, 1930), pp. 26-29.

TABLE II

Group A establishments without miniature *stūpas*	Group B establishments with miniature *stūpas*	Group C establishments with few miniature *stūpas*	Date of the site
	Dharmarājikā		1st cent. B.C.
Chir Tope A			1st-2nd cent.
	Chir Tope B		,,
Chir Tope C			,,
Chir Tope D1			,,
Chir Tope D2			,,
	Kalawan		1st cent.
Kalawan (Monastery H)			2nd cent.
Giri A-B			—
	Giri C-D-E.		—
Kuṇāla			3rd-4th cent.
		Jandial B	1st cent.
		Mohra Moradu	2nd-4th cent.
		Pippala	1st-2nd cent.
	Jaulian		5th cent.
		Lalchak	3rd-4th cent.
	Badalpur		4th cent.
	Bhamala		4th-5th cent.

of rules succeeded in attracting a large number of followers and made Buddhism a popular creed wherein the concepts of *bakti* and *śradhā* were allowed to play their roles. There must have been sects or subsects who did not favour at that time such deviation from the original tenets and discipline of Buddhism; the monasteries of Groups A and C possibly belonged to that orthodox section of Taxila, while the other groups possibly believed in some liberalization of the rules of discipline for the lay-community.

3. APPEARANCE OF BUDDHA-IMAGE

Like the miniature *stūpas* the acceptance of the image of Buddha by various monk-communities did not attain any universality at Taxila. Quite a good number of monasteries there did not yield any human representation of Buddha though the majority of them in some way or the other started image-worship, which appears to have had its beginning some time in the first century A.D. It is evident from Table III (p. 61) that Phase I of Dharmarājikā, Chir Topes A, B, C, D1 and D2, Kalawan (Monastery H), Giri A-B, Kuṇāla monastery and the earliest settlement at Pippala did not reveal any figure of Buddha at all. These monasteries range in date from *circa* first centuary B.C. to the third fourth century A.D., and it is, therefore, certain that the absence of image in these establishments was more due to some ideological factor rather than chronological, more so because the worship of the Master's anthropomorphic form gained considerable popularity in different parts of India by the second-third century A.D. Notwithstanding this popularity a few orthodox schools adhered strictly to the original doctrines of Buddhism; the monasteries referred to above possibly represented those conventional Hīnayāna schools of thought.

The establishment at Dharmarājikā (fig. 16) was, however, quick to absorb this new trend like the Sarvāstivādins residing at Kalawan. At both the places there sprang up a number of image-chapels largely due to the initiative of the lay-worshippers. That a monastic settlement emerged in proximity to the establishment at Kalawan may tend to suggest the existence of a dissident group there who preferred to cling to its original ideals instead of drifting away with the tide of popular urge. At the beginning, the sects with catholic outlook might not have taken the lead themselves in installing Buddha figures; they might have simply allowed the votaries either to construct image-chapels in the monastic precincts or offer images to the *saṅgha*. Thus the chapel G5 of the Dharmarājikā, as the inscription discovered inside it tells, was probably the gift of Urasaka, a Bactrian. Likewise, the inscribed sculptures recovered from the Building L of the same site were for dedication to the *saṅgha* residing at the Dharmarājikā. On the other hand, the minor chapel of Lalchak or Jandial, B site, and an array of shrines around the main *stūpa* at Jaulian (fig. 18) came up as a part of the original lay-out of the settlement. The appearance of Buddha image in different establishments did not, therefore, follow a uniform pattern. In majority of the cases it was in the form of minor chapels, constructed either by the *saṅgha* itself or by the lay-devotees. It must, however, be remembered that nowhere at Taxila the principal *stūpa* was allowed to be overshadowed by the subsidiary edifices except to a certain degree at Kalawan. A compromise must have been arrived at on the relative importance of the principal *stūpa* there *vis-à-vis* Buddha image some time in the fourth-fifth century A.D., when the faces of the main *stūpas* were being decorated with the reliefs of Buddha and the Bodhisattvas: the *stūpas* at Giri C-D-E, Dharmarājikā IV, Mohra-Moradu, Jaulian, Bhamala, Bhallar and, possibly, Badalpur belonged to this movement. One cannot be absolutely sure whether this compromise took place in Gandhāra or elsewhere as this feature is common at many later sites in India. Even the practice of encasing the drum of the *stūpa* with slabs depicting Buddha in human form, as one finds at Amaravati, Nagarjunakonda and Goli, was only a variant of what one finds at Taxila. But exact parallels of this type of *stūpa* come from Ajanta (pl. VII B), Ellora and at many other sites, where the figures of Buddha had been carved out of the rock-cut faces of the *stūpas*. Mention may also be made of the recent discovery of a group of standing Buddha-images on all the four sides of the *stūpa* at Guntapalli, District Krishna, Andhra Pradesh.[1] Basically these are different modes of expression of a common idea which might have evolved at Amaravati and Nagarjunakonda, since at both the places Buddha image made its appearance on the drum-slab definitely by the third centuary A.D., if not earlier. As there is hardly any *stūpa* at Taxila decorated with the representation of the Master prior to the fourth century A.D. the credit of introducing this particular idea should be given to the Āndhrakas. Still, Gandhāra gave this idea a distinctive shape which in subsequent times might have spread to Ajanta, Ellora and other parts of India. Another aspect of this new idea was to shift the sphere of Buddha legend from the rail to the drum of the *stūpa*. At Bharhut, Sanchi, Bodh-Gaya the railing was ear-marked for delineating the story of Buddha—maybe, the *stūpa* remained only as an object of veneration. In the subsequent period the Buddha figures and legends associated with Master's life occupied the *stūpa*-faces which were so long being embellished with simple reliefs like corinthian pillars, etc. It became all the more necessary at Taxila as the principal *stūpas* here had no rails : evidence of railing around minor *stūpas* came only from a few sites like the Dharmarājikā (Stūpas D3 and R1) and Gahi.[2] This transference of Buddha figures from rail to the *stūpa* proper was no small change inasmuch as it developed into a model of synthesis between the anthropomorphic form with the aniconic one of the Master and soon spread far and wide; even the minor *stūpas* were being raised on the same line. By this time the funerary origin of these *stūpas* must have lost sight of in an anxiety to transform them as a symbol of the Great Master.

Yet another feature, though not widespread, was the occurrence of Buddha image inside the monastic residence. Examples of this type of monastery came from Mohra Moradu, Kalawan and Jaulian (fig. 18). Mohra Moradu appears to be an almost Mahāyāna establishment with Buddha figures of superhuman size installed in front of the monastic cells and also in niches. Likewise, each cell of the quadrangular monastery at Jaulian (fig. 18) had alcoves sunk into the façade for figure-sculptures. But at Kalawan images were enshrined in separate cells possibly for the exclusive use of the resident-monks. This development may signify the tendency of some monk-communities to draw a line of demarcation between their own place of worship and that of the lay-worshippers who congregated around the main *stūpa* (below, p. 63). This attitude was shared equally by those who did not favour the worship of the Buddha image. For instance, monastery M 5 and monastic courts A, B and G at the Dharmarājikā, Chir Topes A, B, C and D 2, Pippala etc., had their *stūpas* or *stūpa*-chapels inside the residential areas.[3]

1 *Indian Archaeology—1961-62, A Review*, p, 97, pl. CXXXVII.

2 Ghosh (1948), *op. cit.*. p. 44.

3 For similar developments at Nagarjunakonda see the next chapter.

TABLE III

Classification of monastic establishments at Taxila according to the presence or absence of Buddha image

Establishments without Buddha image	Date	Establisements with Buddha image				Date	Remarks
		minor chapels	within monastery	carved on principal *stūpa*	carved on minor *stūpa*		
Dharmarājikā I	Ist cent. B.C.	Dharmarājikā II	x	x	x	Ist cent A.D.	
Chir Tope A	Ist-2nd cent. A.D.	Dharmarājikā III	x	x	Dharmarājikā III	2nd cent. A.D.	
Chir Tope B	"	Dharmarājikā IV	x	Dharmarājikā IV	Dharmarājikā IV	4th-5th cent. A.D.	
Chir Tope C	"	Kalawan	Kalawan	x	x	1st cent. A.D.	there were later phases as well
Chir Tope D1	"	Giri C-D-E	x	Giri C-D-E	Giri C-D-E	5th cent. A.D.	
Chir Tope D2	"	Jandial	x		x	1st cent. A.D.	
		x	Mohra Moradu.	Mohra Moradu.	Mohra Moradu (*stūpa* inside cell)	2nd cent. A.D.	figure decoration during 4th cent.
Kalawan (Monastery H)	2nd cent. A.D.	x	x	x	Pippala (*stūpa* inside cell)	1st-2nd cent. A.D.	*stūpa* inside the cell quite late
		Jaulian	Jaulian	Jaulian	x	5th cent. A.D.	
Giri A-B	—	Lalchak	x	x	x	3rd-4th cent. A.D.	
Kuṇāla	3rd-4th cent. A.D.	Badalpur	x	Badalpur	x	4th cent. A.D.	
Pippala I	1st cent. A.D.	x	x	Bhamala	Bhamala	4th-5th cent. A.D.	

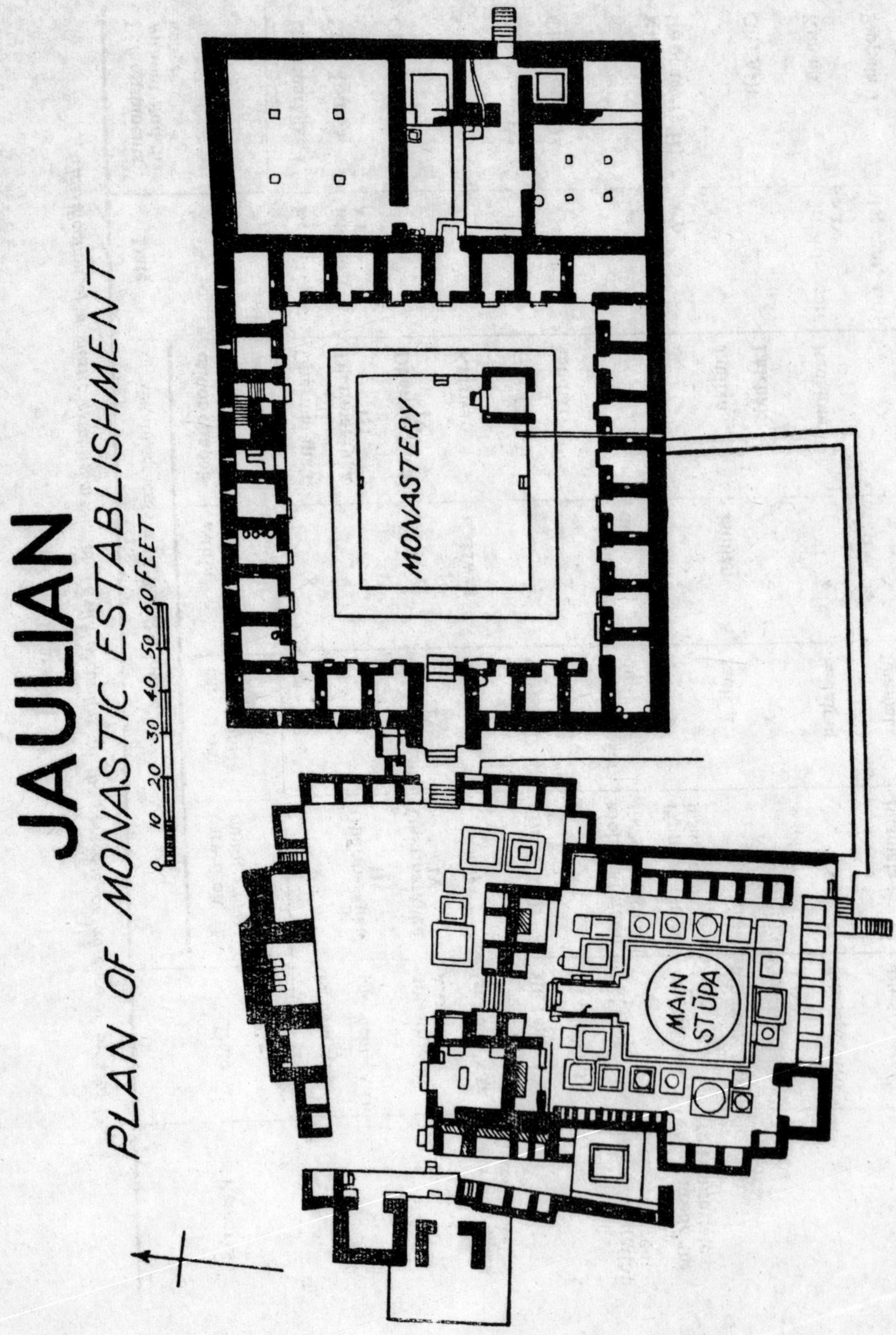
JAULIAN
PLAN OF MONASTIC ESTABLISHMENT
0 10 20 30 40 50 60 FEET
MONASTERY
MAIN STŪPA

FIG. 18

4. THE GṚIHA-STŪPAS

Mention is already made in the preceding chapter (above, pp. 40ff.) about the different varieties of *stūpa*-shrines at Taxila. Suffice here to say that the quadrangular ones achieved maximum popularity, and that the apsidal types, either with semi-circular or octagonal apse (figs. 9 and 13), proved to be a short-lived phenomenon.

However, examples at Taxila, from the point of view of their locations, may be divided into three categories, viz., (i) private *stūpa*-chapels inside the city, (ii) *stūpa*-chapels situated inside the monastic habitation and (iii) those located outside the monastery proper, preferably around the main *stūpa*-complex. In the first category comes the apsidal *stūpa*-shrines from Sirkap (above, p. 53), while quadrangular *gṛiha-stūpas* from Chir Topes B and C, and also possibly Mohra Moradu are to be included in the second category. *Stūpas* of memorial character found inside the monk-cells, examples of which come from Kalawan and Pippala are not to be confused with the quadrangular types mentioned above; incidentally, such memorial *stūpas* bear close similarity with those from the western Indian caves (p. 33). Under the third group falls the apsidal and quadrangular shrines of Dharmarājikā and Kalawan.

The emergence of *gṛiha-stūpa* within the monastic enclosure reflects the anxiety of the resident-monks to have their own place of worship distinct from that of the lay-worshippers (above, p. 60). It is worth noting that no apsidal shrine came up within the residential area of the monk; this feature, however, became quite popular in the Nagarjunakonda valley by the third century. The practice of raising such shrines around the main *stūpas* also assumed wide vogue at Nagarjunkonda but the trend represented by the first category of shrines at Texila is still without any parallel.

As mentioned earlier the apsidal or its cognate form occurred only sporadically in the Taxila region. Perhaps these were only noble attempts by some lay-worshippers to construct shrines of their respective choice. On the contrary, one can easily notice the hands of the *saṅgha* proper in rearing the *stūpa*-chapels of oblong variety, which in the course of time overshadowed all other form to become inseparably associated, specially in the Mahāyānic period, with the image of Buddha.

5. THE PRINCIPAL STŪPAS

The *mahā-chaitya* remained all along the principal monument within a monastic complex from the time of Aśoka down to the fifth century A.D. Such a long period of structural activities must have witnessed several architectural designs and constructional developments, and the Buddhist sects being alive to such changes adopted many of these innovations to make their structures stable, lofty and imposing.

The history of the Dharmarājikā *stūpa* itself records many of these changes brought about as a result of new constructional devices and fresh ideological impetus. Its beginning was like that of any other *stūpa*, with a hemispherical dome resting on a low circular plinth; in fact, such *stūpas* at Dharmarājikā, Manikiala and Jamalgarhi represent the earliest series in Gandhāra. These were all examples of solid constructions, but during the first century A.D., when the Dharmarājikā *stūpa* saw its first major renovation, the solid core was replaced by a wheel-shaped plan. Though not identical but very similar in architectural conception was the one attached to a house at Sirkap where the interior had walls arranged cross-wise as well as diagonally (fig. 19). At Dharmarājikā stūpa, however, the plan was clearly that of a wheel, thereby symbolizing in structural form the idea of *dharma-chakra*.

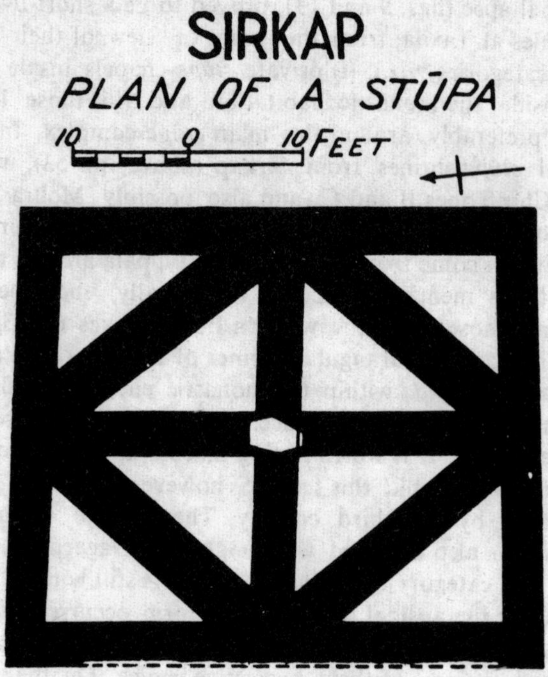

FIG. 19

The Dharmarājikā stūpa (fig. 16) which had an average diameter of 115 feet, was provided with the flights of steps at four cardinal directions during its third phase. But for the *stūpa* at Bhamala no other example at Taxila had flights of steps on all the four sides. Marshall has dated the third phase of the Dharmarājikā to the second century, and it is, therefore, obvious that this feature though introduced quite early at Taxila, did not receive general approval, for generally the *stūpas* at Taxila had only one flight of steps; the Sarvāstivādin monastery at Kalawan did not adopt it at all.

The fourth phase of the Dharmarājikā stūpa attributable to the fourth-fifth century A.D., saw some developments in the interior decoration of the *stūpa*-faces by means of providing ornamental bands above the berm, and niches for the images of Buddha and his attendants. As already stated (p. 59), this feature came into vogue at Taxila some time in the fourth century A.D.—possibly in the wake of strong Mahāyānic influence.

It is evident from the foregoing that the construction of the principal *stūpas* of Taxila did not follow any set track : new features were being evolved or introduced but none of them could make any universal appeal, for either they might not have been compatible with the ideology that a particular sect professed or were considered unnecessary from the point of view of building construction. For example, the wheel-shaped plan in spite of its early origin at Taxila did not find favour with the architects there. The reason for this disfavour was the use of stone as the primary building material; when core could be made solid by means of laying stone blocks, the supply of which was also quite plenty, the builders would hardly feel any necessity to experiment with new methods for making the monuments strong and enduring. Again, in order to raise the height of the *stūpa* the architects of Taxila made use of two methods, viz., the introduction of recessed terraces and elevating the dome on a very high drum, the former became possible because of the adoption of square plinth in place of circular one as early as the beginning of the Christian era, if not earlier. By about the first century A.D. the recessed platforms, as one finds in the construction of the *stūpas* at Chir Topes A, C, D 1 and D 2, and subsequently at Kuṇāla monastery, Lalchak, Badalpur etc., attained considerable popularity. Jandial, Bhamala and Bhallar *stūpas* were, however, built on high drum; in case of the last-mentioned one the drum itself had six or seven tiers. These developments were directed towards giving the *stūpa* a towering height and a majestic appearance. The Dhamek stūpa of Sarnath ascribable to the sixth century A.D., is very similar in architectural conception to that of the Bhallar stūpa. In certain instances, as at Kalawan (fig. 20) and Kuṇāla monasteries, the dome

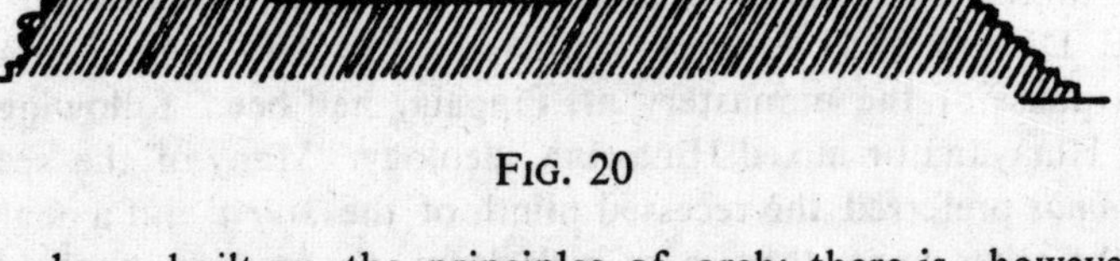

FIG. 20

seemed to have been built on the principles of arch; there is, however, no direct evidence to substantiate the statement but the representation of arches on *stūpa*-faces is likely to suggest their use in actual construction also. Moreover, the existence of the so-called relic-chamber in the centre of the *stūpa* is unexplainable unless they are taken as the lower part of the arch. 'A feature of particular interest in this *stūpa* (stūpa A 4 at Kalawan)' says Marshall,[1] 'is the unusually large size of its circular relic chamber, which is no less than 13 ft. 3 in. in diameter, with walls which start to cove inwards from a height of between 2 and 3 ft. above the floor.' Evidently, when

[1] Marshall (1951), *op. cit.*, pp. 323-24.

the walls show a tendency 'to cove inwards' they are likely to meet with each other at a certain height like that of an arch.

Another peculiarity in the arrangement of the principal *stūpa* at Taxila deserves specific mention: it was the practice among the Buddhists to enclose the *mahā-chaitya* by rows of small image-chapels but it did not in any way assume any great proportions at Taxila in spite of the fact that this was quite a familiar feature in different parts of Gandhāra. Of the monastic establishments, the Dharmārājikā (fig. 16), Giri C-D-E, Chir Tope and Jaulian (fig. 18) had such shrines around the *stūpa*. The minor chapels replacing the ring of miniature *stūpas* at Dharmarājikā had shrines around *stūpa* aligned in the form of a circle, a feature noticed also at Jamalgarhi, whereas the image-chapels of Jaulian, as also of Takt-i-Bahi, were arranged in the shape of a quadrangle. The lay-out, at least in the initial stage, appears to have been confined mainly to the Gandhāra region. Similarly, the cruciform plan of the *stūpa* was more common in the Trans-Indus regions or even beyond the borders than in any other parts of India. At Taxila this type is represented only by the ruins of the Bhamala stūpa (fig. 21). This architectural plan seems to have been introduced quite late in the history of the structural activities as there is not a single *stūpa* of this plan, not even the one at Shahji-ki-Dheri, which can be dated earlier to the fourth-fifth century A.D. It is this form which might have spread to Khotan since the Rawak stūpa there had a plan similar to that of the cruciform *stūpa* of Gandhara.[1] In the Gangetic valley a smaller example of this type was unearthed at Sarnath but the best specimen representing the climax of Buddhist architectural tradition came from Paharpur;[2] the monastery there was built by the Pāla ruler Dharmapāla towards the end of the eighth century.

How far the variations in the form of the principal *stūpa* were due to doctrinal differences is not known. An attempt to classify these establishments on the basis of outward decorations like the appearance of the Buddha image etc.. is made in one of the earlier sections (p. 57), and it would appear therefrom that the authors of the earliest phases of the Dharmarājikā stūpa and Kalawan monastery, besides Chir Topes A, B, C, D1 and D2, Kalawan (monastery H), Giri A-B, Kuṇāla monastery and the early phase of the monastery at Pippala, had been following a faith very similar to the Hīnayāna or mixed Hīnayāna ideology. Many of the sects residing in these *saṅghārāmas* preferred the recessed plinth of the *stūpa* and a flight of steps on one side. On the other hand, the use of high drum, the cruciform plan and flights of steps on all the four sides were absent amongst these orthodox Hīnayānists. These features, however, were introduced quite late in the history of Buddhist architecture, yet it has to be conceded that the Hīnayānists did not try at all to remodel their *stūpas* and *saṅghārāmas* on those lines. From the point of view of *stūpa*-architecture the Hīnayāna monk-establishments referred to above may be divided into two classes, viz., (i) those having recessed plinth and a flight of steps, and (ii) *stūpas*

[1] *Annual Report of the Archaeological Survey of India, 1910-11* (Calcutta 1914).

[2] Percy Brown, *op. cit.*, p. 181.

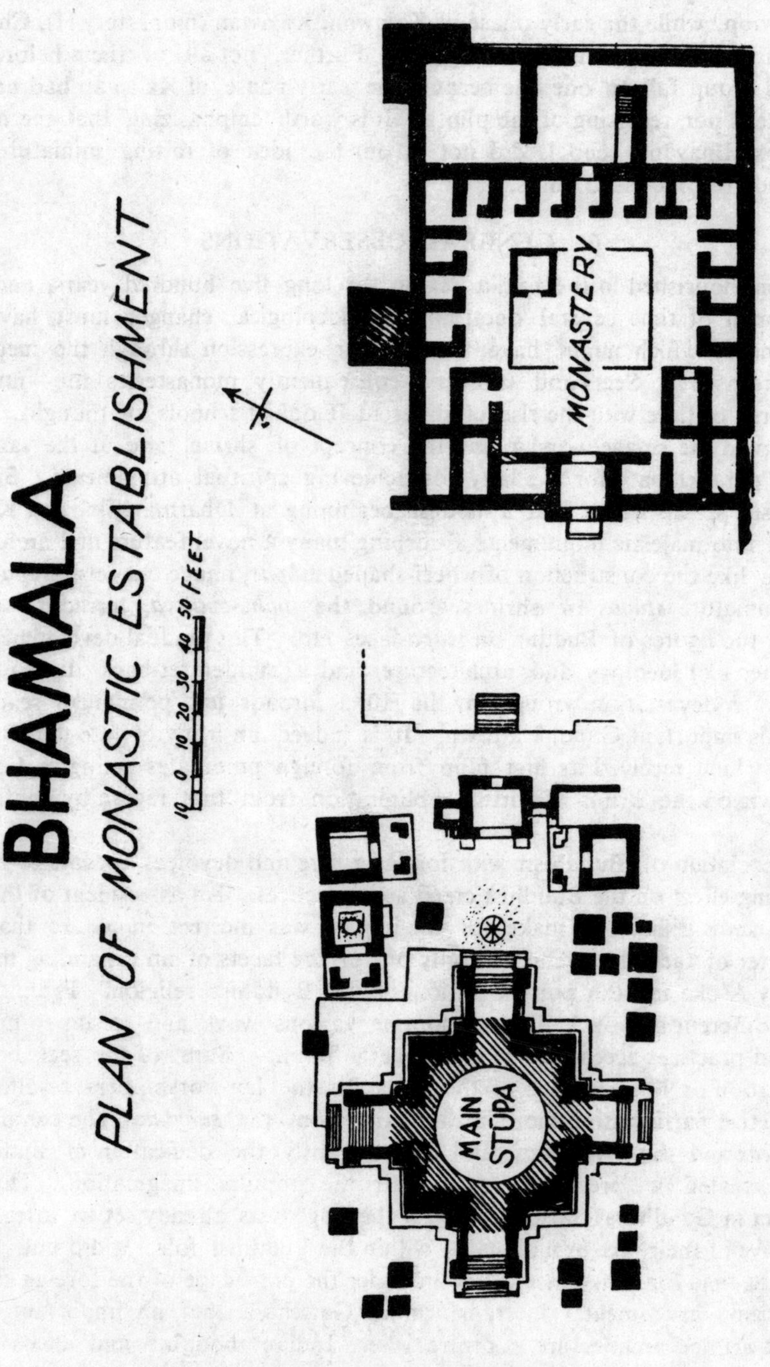
BHAMALA
PLAN OF MONASTIC ESTABLISHMENT
10 0 10 20 30 40 50 FEET
MONASTERY
MAIN STŪPA

FIG. 21

without recessed platform. Chir Topes A, C, D1, D2 and Kuṇāla monastery fall under the first group, while the early phase of Kalawan, Kalawan (monastery H), Chir Tope B and Giri A-B belong to the second group. Further, not all of them belonging to the second group fall on one line because the early phase of Kalawan had neither a flight of steps nor recessing of the plinth. It is worth emphasizing that the majority of orthodox Hīnayāna schools did not favour the idea of raising miniature votive *stūpas* inside the monastic limits.

6. GENERAL OBSERVATIONS

Buddhism flourished in the Taxila region for long five hundred years, and within this vast span of time several doctrinal and ideological changes must have taken place, some of which might have found their expression through the medium of architecture as well. Sects and subsects—consequently monasteries too—multiplied in the course of time with the rise of different Buddhist schools of thought. Several sects accepted the image-worship and the concept of shrine, and at the same time, evolved a parallel path for the laity for achieving spiritual attainments. Similarly, the monastic set-up which had a modest beginning at Dharmarājikā and Kalawan, developed into majestic monuments absorbing many a novel feature and architectural innovation like the construction of wheel-shaped *stūpas*, image-chapels, *stūpa*-shrines, ring of miniature *stūpas* or shrines around the *mahā-chaitya*, terraced *stūpa* and carving of the figures of Buddha on *stūpa*-faces etc. This gradual developments both in the spheres of ideology and architecture had a sudden set-back during the fifth century when devastation wrought by the Hūṇa inroads left permanent scars on the face of this important Gandhāra town. It is indeed an irony of fate that Buddhism at Taxila which received its first fillip from foreign potentates ruling in Gandhāra, was thrown on the brink of virtual obliteration from that region by another alien folk.

The association of Buddhism with foreign rulers and devotees appears to have had far-reaching effect on the Buddhist creed and practices. An assessment of this aspect of Buddhism is difficult to make, for the impact was indirect in nature than direct. As a matter of fact, this trend was only one of the facets of an expanding movement started by Aśoka for the popularization of the Buddhist religion. From that time onwards different schools had been adopting various ways and means to make their tenets and practices acceptable to the general public. Some of the sects believed in the relaxation or liberalization of the rules for the lay-worshippers resulting in the latter's active participation more in the activities of the *saṅgha*. The compilation of the *Jātakas* and the *Avadānas*, and concomitantly the deification of Buddha, had already created a precondition to stir the popular imagination. Thus, when Buddhism in Gandhāra started its career the stage was already set to attract people irrespective of their race or nationality within the Buddhist fold. It did not, therefore, take much time for resurgence to set in under the patronage of the foreign rulers who soon became instrumental in transforming Gandhāra into an important centre of Buddhist art and architecture, a centre where Indian thoughts and ideals had their expression largely through an occidental art-idiom. This process of harmonization manifested itself greatly in the exterior embellishments of the *stūpas* and other Buddhist monuments. But this synthesis in the domain of art and architecture is perhaps an outcome of certain collective outlook of the people who influenced directly or indirectly the philosophical and doctrinal aspects of Buddhism too.

It is not a sheer coincidence that the earliest records of this region are replete with references to the donations by the *Yavanas* for constructions of *stūpas*, *saṅghārāmas*, shrines, etc. That Buddhism soon absorbed certain individualistic tendencies also instead of pursuing the corporate ideals of the original Buddhist teachings must have been due to the favour shown to the royal laity, and the Buddhist church from a very early period framed special rules and regulations for the ruling section.[1] Thus, settlements without any *saṅghārāma* in contravention to the normal practices, came into existence in the Saka-Parthian city (above, p. 55); even individual gifts by lay-worshippers often accompanied by loud advertisements, as the labels and inscriptions show, are only expressions of the same individualistic spirit, which must have been exploited by different Buddhist sects to serve ultimately their own purpose, their primary aim being to forge ahead along the road to popularity with more and more larger bands of followers. Not that all the sects or subsects had this passion to gain prominence, for there are a few monasteries at Taxila where neither any image nor any votive *stūpa* was discovered. Evidently, these sects must have strove hard to adhere scrupulously to the original practices even at the risk of getting unpopular. A few tried to maintain a line of demarcation between their own practices and those of the lay-worshippers: in such establishments there were at least two places of worship, one within the monastery for the monks and the other around the principal *stūpa* for the votaries.

The archaeological records of Taxila have left only a few names of sects; hence, the sectarian affiliation of the vast majority of the Buddhist establishments remains unknown. It seems, however, that the Sarvāstivādins formed the most dominant school in the Taxila region at least during the early Christian era, as the name of this sect occurs not only at Kalawan but also in the inscriptions discovered at Shah-ji-ki-Dheri, Zeda, Kurram, Tor Dheri, Mathurā, Śrāvastī and Sarnath. Originally this sect had its nucleus at Mathurā wherefrom it spread far and wide; it is not unlikely that their establishment at Mathurā grew into great proportions because of the patronage of the Śaka satraps. Even its popularity in the Gandhāra region was due to the assistance extended by the foreign rulers and *Yavana* lay-worshippers for the cause of propagation of Buddhism. Particularly favourable for this sect was the period of Kanishka's rule, as the majority of the inscribed documents mentioning the name of the sect are dated to that period, and it was during Kanishka's rule that this sect extended its sphere of influence beyond Gandhāra and Mathurā regions to have settlements as far east as Sarnath. The use of grammatical Sanskrit as the medium of

[1] Dutt (1930), *op. cit.*, p. 300.

their literature was also dictated by the necessity of establishing contact with the foreign rulers and lay-devotees.

The Sarvāstivādins must have started their career as an orthodox Buddhist school professing an ideology very similar to that of the Hīnayānists—the earliest phase of the monastery at Kalawan comprising a *mahā-chaitya* and a *saṅghārāma* possibly representing the typical establishment of that period. However, not much is known about their monastery at Mathurā although it appears from the lion-capital inscriptions of the time of Rañjuvula and Soḍāsa that the establishment there also consisted of a *stūpa* and a *saṅghārāma*, besides *dvaja-stambhas*. Within a few decades their monastery at Kalawan developed into a big settlement, with *gṛiha-stūpas* and image-shrines added to it. This was the only monastery at Taxila where the principal *stūpa* was allowed to be overshadowed by subsidiary structures. Again, this was one of the three sites at Taxila where the apsidal *stūpa*-shrines around the main *stūpa* came up, the other two sites being the Dharmarājikā stūpa and the city-site of Sirkap.

There is no direct evidence as yet to ascribe the Dharmarājikā site to any sect, but on the grounds of some circumstantial evidence it may possibly be ascribed to the Sarvāstivādins. It is a well-known fact that the image of Buddha was first modelled at Mathurā and in Gandhāra, both being the strongholds of the Sarvāstivādins. As a corollary can it not be assumed that it was the Sarvāstivādins who first took to image-worship? As this was the most dominant sect in both the regions during the first century A.D. no other sect could have a better claim for introducing the Master's anthropomorphic form than the Sarvāstivādins. It was also this sect which attributed to Buddha divine or supernatural powers (below, p. 72) in spite of the fact that, like the Theravādins, they too considered Buddha as a human being. From Mathurā and Gandhāra the practice of image-worship spread to Śrāvastī and Sarnath, at least the inscriptions of friar Bala would make this point quite clear.

If it is admitted that the settlement of the Dharmarājikā site belonged to the Sarvāstivādins, a question arises as to the necessity for having another establishment of the same sect at Kalawan. The latter possibly belonged to a dissident group who branched off for some reason or the other from the main stem of the Sarvāstivādins residing at the former site; the Monastery H of Kalawan appears to be a settlement of those monks who did not subscribe to the idea of image worship till to the last days of their stay at Taxila. That this sect was divided into different schools of thought may be affirmed from the expositions by Bhadanta Dharmatrāta, Bhadanta Ghoshaka, Bhadanta Vasumitra and Bhadanta Buddhadeva;[1] it is, however, not known whether such differences led to *saṅgha-bheda*.

Also there were other sects, and some of them must have been the off-shoots of the Sarvāstivādins. For instance, the Kāśyapīyas who came out from the Sarvāstivāda school, must have had a settlement at Taxila also, besides the one at Bedadi, 60 miles to the north of the city, because the Uttarārāma monastery referred to in the copper ladle inscription should normally be situated within the limits of Taxila. The

[1] Dutt (1955), *op. cit.*, II, pp. 145-47.

inscribed ladle came to light from Sirkap, thereby indicating the existence of a Kāśyapīya establishment during the life-time of the second city. Further, the Uttarārāma or the 'northern monastery' is to be sought towards the northern part of the city, and the only monastery in this area datable to the first century A.D. is the one recovered at Jandial, which possessed from its early days an image-shrine attached to a monastic wing. Next to the Sarvāstivādins, the Kāśyapīyas seemed to have a wider sphere of influence, for inscriptions allude to the existence of at least three monasteries, viz., Taxila, Bedadi and Paladu Dheri within Gandhāra and its neighbouring countries;[1] if the reading of the Kāśyapīyas in the Pabhosa cave inscription[2] is correct this sect had its establishment also near Kauśāmbī in the Ganga plane (see, however, Chapter VI).

Another sect, the Sautrāntikas, might have had its centre at Taxila; it was in the monastery attached to the Bhallar stūpa, says Hiuen Tsang,[3] that Kumaralabdha, the founder of the school, composed his treatises. The archaeological remains, the detailed report on which is also not available, do not throw any light so as to corroborate this tradition.

Thus the inscriptions from Taxila mention the existence of at least two sects, viz., the Sarvāstivādins and the Kāśyapīyas, whereas the archaeological ruins bespeak the continuity of an orthodox Sarvāstivāda school who preferred to stick to older teachings and practices. Whether they should be correlated with the Mūla-Sarvāstivādins of the Buddhist text or some other school is quite difficult to say. If the tradition recorded by Hiuen Tsang is based on historical truth one may also assume the existence of another sect, the Sautrāntikas, at Taxila. This school was opposed to the Buddhist cardinal doctrine of the momentary existence of *skandhas*, and admitted the transference of *skandha-mātras* from one existence to another, as the Sammitīyas believed in the transference of *pūdgala* or personality.[4]

All these developments, as stated above, show how different Buddhist doctrines had been undergoing radical changes deviating from the original philosophical expositions of Buddha. This was, in fact, a period of crystalization of the Mahāyānic doctrines of Buddhism which had their germinations in the tenets of the older schools like the Sarvāstivādins and the Mahāsāṅghikas. Unfortunately the monastic architecture of Taxila failed to offer any clue on the existence of Mahāyānic monks. Actually the distinction between a Mahāyānic establishment of its formative period and that of the Hīnayānists appears to be quite undefined because all the ideas with the exception of the concept of *dharma-śuṇyatā* had their emergence in the doctrines of the Hīnayāna sects; both the Sarvāstivādins and the Mahāsāṅghikas might have contributed equally to the rise of the Mahāyānic ideals and practices. It is, however, generally assumed on the basis of scriptural evidence that the Mahāsāṅghikas or their

1 Sten Konow, *op. cit.*, p. cxvii.

2 *Epigraphia Indica*, II, p. 242 ff.

3 Thomas Watters, *On Yuan Chwang's Travels in India (A.D. 629-645)* (Delhi, 1961), p. 245.

4 Dutt (1945), *op. cit*, pp. 166-67.

cognate schools first conceived Buddha docetically and the Lokottaravādins, a branch of the Mahāsāṅghikas, gave a final touch to it. On the other hand, the conception of Bodhisattva, the practice of six *pāramitās* and the *Avadāna* literature were not the monopoly of the Mahāsāṅghikas alone, for the Sarvāstivādins also subscribed to these ideals from a very early period. The *Lalita-vistāra*, the biography of Buddha as adopted by the Mahāyānists, originally belonged to the Sarvāstivādins; so far as the archaeological evidence is concerned the Sarvāstivādins by about the first century A.D. evolved the idea of Bodhisattva and gave Buddha an iconic form too. On the contrary there is as yet no archaeological proof to show that the Mahāsāṅghikas or their allied school took recourse to image worship prior to the second century A.D: the drum-slabs of Amaravati stūpa ascribable to the reign of Vāśishṭhīputra Pulumāyi bear only a few figures of Buddha, and that no such sculpture from Nagarjunakonda can be dated earlier to the third century A.D. In the circumstances, the Sarvāstivādins may be acclaimed as a pioneer in the introduction of the anthropomorphic form of the Great Master. At the same time, these developments may indicate the prevalence of the semi-Mahāyānic conceptions in varying degrees amongst different sects of Gandhāra and Taxila. The tradition that Kanishka took active participation in the Fourth Buddhist Council for settling the disputes between the Hīnayānists and the Mahāyānists would presuppose the presence of a good number of monks adhering to the Mahāyānic principles in Gandhāra and in the neighbouring provinces, and, as this region was the home of the Sarvāstivādins, who also received Kanishka's patronage, they were none else but the Sarvāstivādin monks advocating Mahāyānic doctrines. These monks had been practising six *pāramitās* and believed in the extraordinary powers and knowledge of the Buddhas; maybe, the monastery with giant images at Mohra Moradu was the creation of such a group. Still, it has to be admitted that the existence of a full-fledged Mahāyānic settlement at Taxila is quite doubtful.

It will be a misrepresentation of facts if the Mahāsāṅghikas are excluded altogether as one of the forerunners of the Mahāyānism. They must have also played a role in the development of this philosophy; indeed, this sect had their settlement in north-western India even as early as the first century A.D., at least the mention of the Mahāsāṅghikas in the Mathurā lion-pillar capital inscriptions carries such an impression. Moreover, their settlement at Wardak is a sure proof of their foothold in that country. Taking all these facts into account one can hardly deny the presence of the Mahāsāṅghika monks upholding Mahāyānic principles even in the Gandhāra region. This new doctrine, therefore, might have owed their origin mainly to two different groups of monks originally belonging either to the Mahāsāṅghika or Sarvāstivāda schools. The fact that Mahāyānism flourished in eastern India does not necessarily mean that this new doctrine was formulated in that region itself: had there been no Hūṇa invasion Taxila could have easily developed itself into a true Mahāyānic centre. Truly speaking, it was the political condition rather than any other factor which might have determined the course of Mahāyānic movement in India.

Thus, Taxila which started its career as the true Hīnayānists, with the Sarvāstivādins as the most dominant sect, paved the ground for the Mahāyānism to rise. From the beginning of the Christian era different sects at Taxila had been pursuing an ideal very much akin to what the scholars term as mixed Hīnayāna doctrines.[1] Their architecture and plastic art reflect a state of flux when various sects instead of perpetrating the teachings of Buddha had been drifting away from the original moorings to adjust their doctrines and practices according to the tide of the popular urge, and also more often than not, in consonance with the mood of the privileged section, including the royalty. The striking similarity in the popular conception of Buddhism, as the donative records display, between Taxila and Nagarjunakonda at once brings out the universal trend shared both by the Sarvāstivādins and the Mahāṅsāghikas; it is nothing else but their craving for popularity, consequently their tendency to relax and liberalize the rules of discipline at the cost of sacrificing the original teachings of Buddha. In other words, it was the collective psychology of the people which had been, to a great extent, shaping the destiny of Buddhist movement in India, not to speak of Taxila.

[1] Dutt (1930), *op. cit.*, pp. 4 ff.

CHAPTER FIVE

NAGARJUNAKONDA

The large-scale excavation at Nagarjunakonda carried out by the Archaeological Survey of India during the years 1954-60,[1] have added considerably to the number of Buddhist establishments exposed there earlier by Longhurst[2] and Ramachandran.[3] The total number of such establishments (fig. 22), all of the third-fourth centuries A.D., is now about over thirty, and they belong to different sects. In detail they vary from each other, but no attempt has so far been made to find out whether such variations are due to idiosyncrasy or chronology or are inherent in the ideology of the sect to which the establishment belonged.

Nagarjunakonda flourished at an epoch when the doctrines of different Buddhist sects were in the crucible—consequent on the impact of popular beliefs and practices on original teachings of Buddha. Despite the fact that the Buddhist edifices of Nagarjunakonda were constructed more than hundred years after the Fourth Buddhist Council, the majority of the sects had been following a faith not exactly similar to the Mahāyāna doctrine. Some of them were offshoots of the Mahāsāṅghikas, whose philosophical beliefs stood in contrast to Mahāyāna. The deification of Buddha in Āndhra-deśa started with the Mahāsāṅghikas and the allied schools; and this movement, reinforced by the conception of *śūnyatā*, etc., culminated in Mahāyānism, which, according to Dutt,[4] had its seed in the doctrines of different sects of Āndhra-deśa like the Lokottaravādin, Apara-mahāvina-seliya, Bahuśrutīya, etc (above, p. 72).

It would appear from the history of structural activities, coupled with epigraphs,[5] that different sects made this picturesque valley their happy abode. Inscriptions affirm the existence of at least four sects, viz., Mahāvihāra-vāsin, Mahī-śāsaka, Bahuśrutīya and Apara-mahāvina-seliya; the last one, being the most dominant sect, has left behind it a number of records to vouch its superior status. There might have been other sects or groups of dissenters, but their names are not available. It is obvious from the

[1] The excavations were done under Dr. R. Subrahmanyam assisted by others including the present author. See H. Sarkar and B. N. Mishra, *Nagarjunakonda* (New Delhi, 1966).

[2] A. H. Longhurst, *The Buddhist Antiquities of Nagarjunakonda, Madras Presidency*, Mem. Arch. Surv. Ind., no. 54 (1938).

[3] T. N. Ramachandran, *Nagarjunakonda*, 1938, Mem. Arch. Surv. Ind., no. 71 (1953).

[4] Nalinaksha Dutt (1945), *op, cit.*, II, p. 41.

[5] For Buddhist inscriptions of Nagarjunakonda, see J. Ph. Vogel in *Epigraphia Indica*, XX (1929-30), pp. 1-37, and XXI (1931-32), pp. 61-71; D. C. Sircar in *ibid*, XXXIII (1959-61), pp. 247-50, XXXIV (1961-62), pp. 197 ff. and XXXV (1963-64), pp. 1-36; H. Sarkar in *ibid.*, XXXVI (1964-65), pp. 273-74.

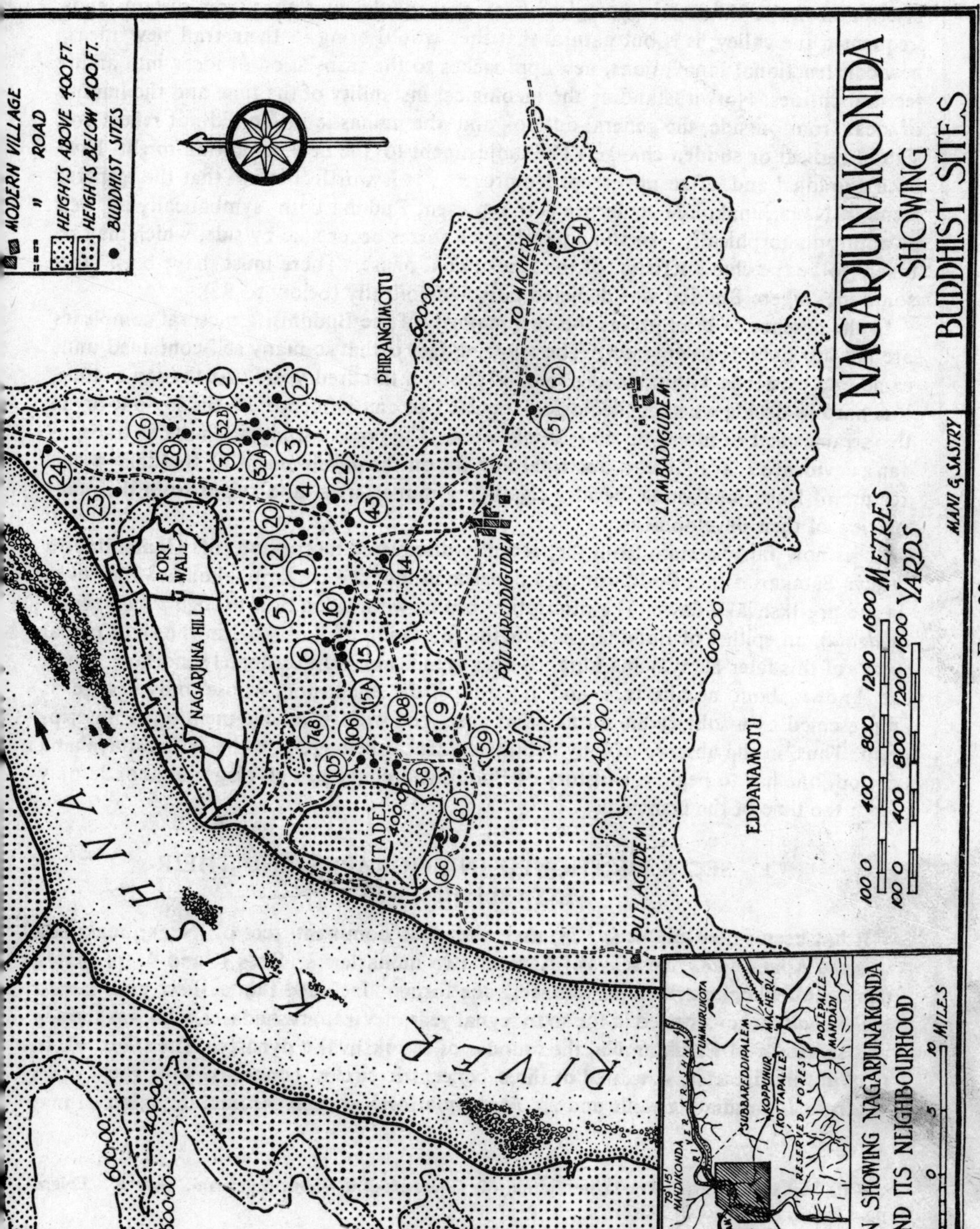
NAGARJUNAKONDA
SHOWING
BUDDHIST SITES
MODERN VILLAGE
" ROAD
HEIGHTS ABOVE 400 FT.
HEIGHTS BELOW 400 FT.
BUDDHIST SITES
1000 400 800 1200 1600 METRES
1000 400 800 1200 1600 YARDS
MANI & SASTRY
PLAN SHOWING NAGARJUNAKONDA
AND ITS NEIGHBOURHOOD
5 0 5 10 MILES
RIVER KRISHNA
NAGARJUNA HILL
FORT WALL
CITADEL
PHIRANGIMOTU
TO MACHERLA
PULLAREDDIGUDEM
LAMBADIGUDEM
EDDANAMOTU
PUTLAGUDEM
600.00
400.00
NANDIKONDA
RAYAVARAM
TUMMURUKOTA
SUBBAREDDIPALEM
MACHERLA
KOPPUNUR
KOTTAPALLE
RESERVED FOREST
POLEPALLE
MANDADI
AREA OF MAP

FIG. 22

inscription in the Chula-Dhaṁmagiri-vihāra that monks and nuns from distant lands frequented the valley; it is but natural that they would bring in their trail new ideas, new constructional innovations, new approaches to the translation of ideas into architectural entities. Notwithstanding the ideological instability of the time and the import of ideas from outside, the general outlook and the monastic set-up did not reflect any sign of radical or sudden change. The adjustment to the new condition might have been a gradual and often imperceptible process. It is worth noting that the general trend of Nagarjunakonda sculpture is to represent Buddha both symbolically as well as anthropomorphically. In some panels such forms occur side by side, which may be taken to be the characteristic of the transitional phase. There must have been also some sites where Buddha was depicted only symbolically (below p. 95).

In the absence of inscriptions the vast majority of the Buddhist structural complexes are not attributable to any sect. The amazing fact is that so many self-contained units came into existence within a short span of about a hundred years. At the same time, it is hard to decide whether ideological beliefs had any influence on the lay-out or in the arrangement of monastic units in all cases. The present study attempts to trace, as far as evidence is available, a doctrinal imprint on the development of Buddhist architecture of Nagarjunakonda, besides classifying monasteries and *stūpas* from the point of view of their development.

It is now fairly certain from the recently-discovered inscription of Gautamīputra Vijaya Sātakarṇī[1] that Buddhism had penetrated into the Nagarjunakonda valley even in the pre-Ikshvāku days. The inscription begins with salutation to *aga-pogali* (*agra-pudgala*), an epithet of Buddha; the date the full-moon of Vaiśākha, in the sixth regnal year of this later Sātavāhana king, is also significant. Unfortunately, nothing could be known about architecture and lay-out of the monastery whose only vestige is represented by a solitary limestone pillar inscribed with the above-mentioned inscription. Thus, in the absence of any definite evidence belonging to the later Sātavāhana period, one has to begin the history of Buddhist architecture of Nagarjunakonda only from the time of the Ikshvākus.

1. SECTS MENTIONED IN EPIGRAPHS AND THEIR ESTABLISHMENTS

It has been stated above (p. 74) that the most dominant sect of Nagarjunakonda was the Apara-mahāvina-seliyas. At least two monasteries, Sites 1 and 9 (pl. XIII), can definitely be ascribed to this sect; the former included the earliest and largest *mahā-chaitya*, constructed in the sixth regnal year of Vīrapurushadatta, who was the son and successor of Chāṁtamūla, the founder of the Ikshvāku dynasty. The *stūpa*, 91 ft. (27·7m.) in diameter, consisted of three concentric circles connected with each other by cross and radiating walls and an *āyaka*-platform at each cardinal direction. It may

1 H. Sarkar, 'Nagarjunakonda inscription of Gautamiputra Vijaya Satakarni, year 6', *Epigraphia Indica*, XXXVI, pp. 273-74.

be inferred from inscriptions[1] that at first only the *mahā-chaitya* was built and the monastery was added in the fifteenth regnal year of the same king. In his eighteenth year came into being a *chaitya-gṛiha* enshrining a *stūpa*.

The other monastery, Site 9 (pl. VIII A), was definitely renovated, if not constructed, in the eighth regnal year of Ehuvala Chāṁtamūla, the son of Vīrapurushadatta.[2] It was a self-sufficient unit, with more than one phase, having a *mahā-chaitya*, two *chaitya-gṛihas* and a three-winged monastery. A rubble *stūpa* with a *vihāra*, built on earth-fast poles, belonged to the earliest phase. But the *chaitya-gṛiha* to set up a Buddha-image and two votive *stūpas* in front of the other apsidal shrine were important accretions not encountered in the earlier monastery of the Apara-mahāvina-seliyas (Site 1). This may indicate that this sect started its activities in the valley at a time when the worship of the Buddha-image was not in its tenets: the main object of worship was the *mahā-chaitya*, the *stūpa* enshrined in the *chaitya-gṛiha* being secondary. The original sect living in Site 1 thus did not accept the idea of image-worship till the end. On the other hand, the Buddha-image did find place in the other monastery, Site 9. Thus, it may safely be concluded that the Apara-mahāvina-seliyas of Nagarjunakonda became divided into two sub-sects. Site 17, popularly known as Hāritī temple overlooking the giant Amphitheatre, also yielded an inscription[3] mentioning the name of the Apara-mahāvina-seliya sect, who had possibly another settlement either at the very site or near by.

The monastery situated on the Chula-Dhaṁmagiri, Site 43 (pl. XIII), may be attributed to the Theravādin monks of Ceylon. Here, in the fourteenth regnal year of Vīrapurushadatta a female lay-worshipper from Govagāma, Bodhiśrī by name, built a *chaitya-gṛiha* with a *stūpa*—the first of its kind in the ancient city of Vijayapurī. The main *stūpa* of the site, with a circular rim made of brick, had a solid rubble-core, without spokes or *āyaka*-platforms. This sect did not possibly yield to the idea of the worship of Buddha in the beginning: nor did they follow the tradition of the construction of *stūpa* with a wheel-base and *āyaka*-platforms. But at a later stage even an oblong shrine with a pedestal, evidently for an image, was added inside the residential enclosure.

Another Ceylonese sect, the Mahāvihāra-vāsin, established a monastery, Site 38, (pl. IX A), as is known from the undated inscription on a Buddha-pāda found here.[4]

1 All the epigraphs inscribed on the *āyaka*-pillars bear an identical date, viz., the tenth day of the sixth rainy season of the sixth regnal year of Vīrapurushadatta. It is, therefore, likely that that day witnessed the consecration of this gigantic *stūpa*, which does not appear to have had any earlier nucleus. *Nava-kaṁma*, mentioned in the inscriptions, may mean 'new construction,' not 'reconstruction', *Ep. Ind.*, XX, p. 30. The Chula-Dhaṁmagiri inscription states: *imaṁ nava-kaṁmaṁ tiṁhi navaka* [*ṁ*]*-mikehi kāritaṁ*. It is difficult to believe that a class of masons did only renovation. Cf. *Chullavagga*, VI, 5, 2 and 3, Sacred Books of the East, XX (1885), pp. 190-91.

2 *Indian Archaeology 1957-58—A Review* (1958), pp. 8-9.

3 *Epigraphia Indica, XXXIV*, pp. 210-11.

4 *Ep. Ind.* XXXIII (1960), p. 249. The editors of the inscription are inclined to interpret the word *mahāvihāra-vāsin* as 'the residents of the *mahāvihāra*' attached to the Great Stūpa (Site 1). But that *mahāvihāra* definitely belonged to the Apara-mahāvina-seliyas. Moreover, Site 38, where the foot-print slab was discovered, was more than a mile away from Site 1.

The construction of the main *stūpa* of this monastery was on the lines of those at Site 43: it was of brick but without any *āyaka*-platform and was, further, not wheel-shaped on plan. In a later phase the monastery was embellished with a *chaitya-gṛiha*, but it is not certain whether this apsidal shrine was meant for an image of Buddha or for the worship of the Buddha-pāda, which was discovered at the site itself. A number of votive *stūpas* around the main *stūpa* came into existence in a still subsequent phase. Thus, the Mahāvihāra-vāsins launched upon their career like the orthodox Theravādins but gradually assimilated the idea of constructing votive *stūpas* and also possibly of Buddha-worship. This monastery therefore differs from the Chula-Dhaṁmagiri-vihāra in the existence of a votive *stūpa* and the absence of an apsidal structure enshrining a *stūpa*. These two sites were not identical in their general plan too: Site 38 (pl. IX A) had a *stūpa* as well as a *chaitya-gṛiha*, situated within the residential enclosure. It is not easy to ascribe the Chula-Dhaṁmagiri-vihāra to the Mahāvihāra-vāsins; some other Ceylonese sect was possibly responsible for its construction.

The monastery of the Mahīśāsakas, Site 7-8 (pl. XIII), was built by the sister of Ehuvala Chāṁtamūla and queen of Vanavāsi in the eleventh regnal year of Ehuvala. Vanavāsi was one of the main centres of the Mahīśāsaka sect,[1] which ideologically was nearer the Theravādins than the Mahāsāṅghikas. The monastery had two large *stūpas* but no *chaitya-gṛiha*. It is, therefore, evident that this sect was averse to *chaitya-gṛihas*, not to speak of image-worship. One of the *stūpas* at the site was wheel-shaped, and both had *āyaka*-platforms.

The second regnal year of Ehuvala Chāṁtamūla saw the construction of another monastery, Site 5 (pl. XIII), for the *āchāryas* of the Bahuśrutīya sect, which had branched off from the Mahāsāṅghikas and, as scholars believe, attempted a syncretism of Hīnayāna and Mahāyāna thoughts. In this monastery there were two *chaitya-gṛihas*, both of them meant for enshrining *stūpas* but not Buddhas. At a slightly later date at least one oblong shrine (pl. IX B) with a decorated pillar in front, simulating a *dhvaja-stambha*, came into existence within the residential part of the monastery. The pillar portrays the figure of a seated Buddha.

It is apparent from the foregoing that the sects did not have identical types of establishments and that ideological differences manifested themselves in monastic architecture. It is definite that the Apara-mahāvina seliyas did not originally own the idea of worship of Buddha-image. Even the *chaitya-gṛiha* was adopted by them at a slightly later stage. But within a short period of two decades or so, one of their branches came to accept not only the *chaitya-gṛiha* but also the idea of the worship of Buddha and the erection of votive *stūpas*. The Mahīśāsakas resisted these innovations down to their last days in the valley. The Bahuśrutīyas subscribed to the conception of *chaitya-gṛiha* from the very beginning and raised two identical structures each enshrining a *stūpa*. The worship of the Buddha-image was not originally practised by them, but their subsequent history shows that they also fell in line with the Apara-mahāvina-seliyas.

[1] Dutt, *op. cit.*, p. 114.

All the three sects built *stūpas* with *āyaka*-platforms. But the Ceylonese sects did not adopt this constructional feature at all: their *stūpas* had solid bases and were without *āyakas*. The sect which had its monastery on the Chula-Dhaṁmagiri also submitted to the popular demand of image-worhip. The Mahāvihāra-vāsins too were swayed by this new current, but in the *stūpa*-construction both of them struck to the older style. One point needs emphasis: many sects started their careers in the valley without the Buddha-image, but most of them succumbed to the idea after a period of resistance or hesitation. This change was effected within a maximum period of a century.

2. CLASSIFICATION OF THE ESTABLISHMENTS

Broadly speaking, the Buddhist establishments of Nagarjunakonda (fig. 22; pl. XIII) may be divided into following five groups.

A. Unit consisting of stupa and monastery

The sites under this group (pl. XIII), Sites 6, 7-8, 14, 15, 20, 21, 27 (pl. X A), 30, 32 A, 32 B, 54 and 86 and the early phases of a few others, may further be divided into two sub-groups of monasteries, viz. (i) those having a *stūpa* with *āyaka*-platforms and (ii) those having a *stūpa* without *āyaka*-platform. Sites 6, 7-8, 14,[1] 20, 21, 30, 32 A, 54 and 86 were associated with *stūpas* having *āyaka*-platforms at the four cardinal directions. None of them, except Sites 7-8, 14 and 54, had a central hall or pillared *maṇḍapa*. The second sub-group is represented by Sites 15, 27 (fig. 23) and 32 B. Similarly, the early phase of Site 1 would fall under sub-group (i) and those of Sites 38 and 43 under sub-group; (ii) in all of them the *chaitya-gṛiha* was absent in the early phase.

The simple monastic unit at Nagarjunakonda therefore consisted only of a *stūpa* and a monastery, though there is hardly any reason to assume that such a unit would invariably suggest a chronological priority. It is fairly certain that sects responsible for these units did not uphold the worship of Buddha or the construction of a *chaitya-gṛiha*, all importance being laid on the *stūpa* or *chaitya* itself. It is significant that at least two units of sub group (ii), viz. Sites 38 and 43, belonged, according to inscriptions, to sects of Theravādin affiliation; hence it is not unlikely that the other three units of this sub-group, viz., Sites 15, 27 and 32 B, where there are no inscriptions, also belonged to such sects. The units of sub-group (i) obviously belonged to the other catholic sects not averse to innovations. The Mahīśāsakas, who were the authors of Site 7-8, did not yield to the idea of either image-worship or *chaitya-gṛiha* and preferred two large *stūpas* instead.

B. Unit consisting of stupa, monastery and chaitya-griha with stupa

This group is represented by only eight establishments, viz. Sites 1 (later phase),

[1] This site had an earlier phase, represented by extant remains of another *stūpa* without any *āyaka*-platform.

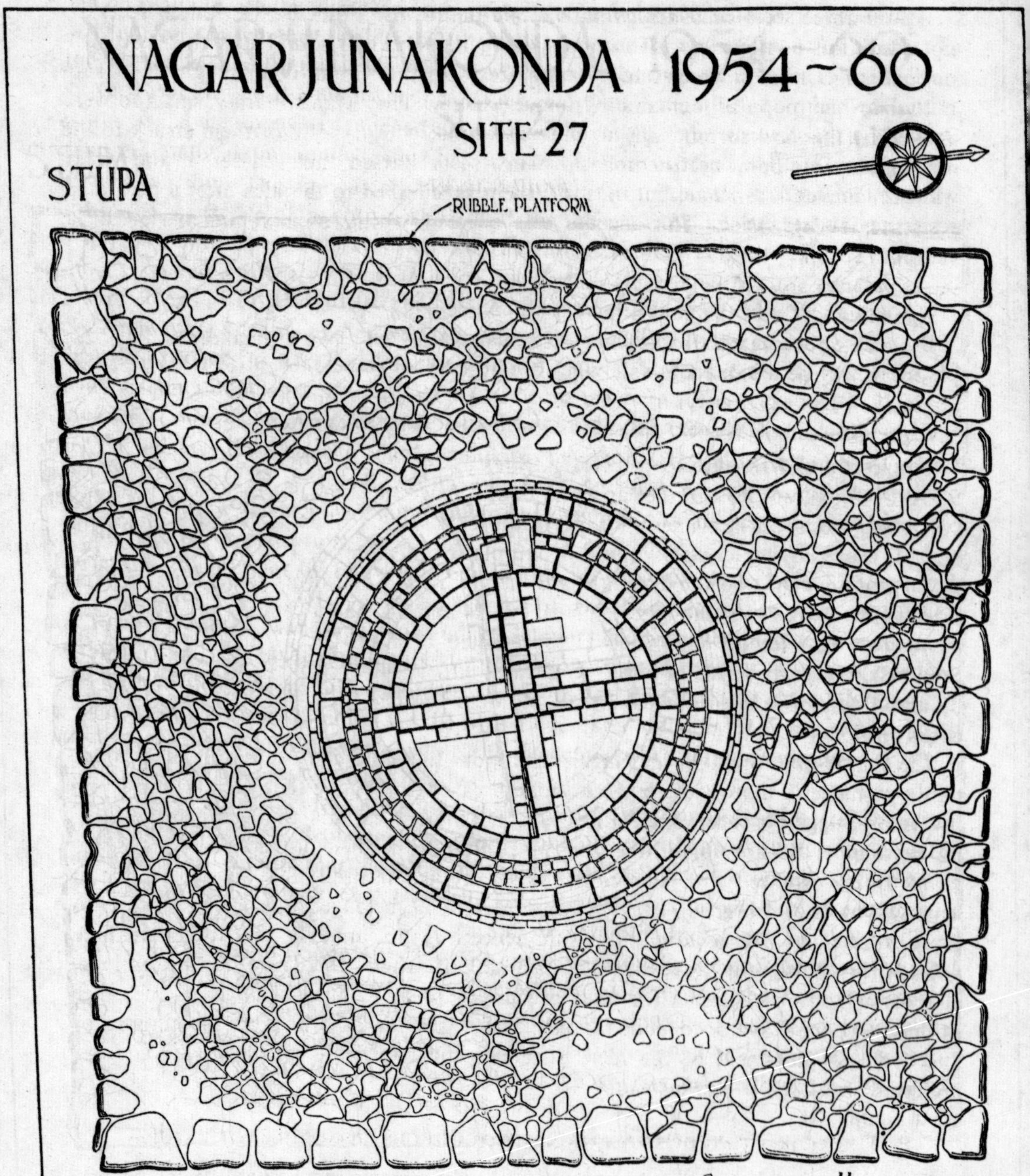
NAGARJUNAKONDA 1954-60
SITE 27
STŪPA
RUBBLE PLATFORM
SCALE OF FEET
1 0 1 2 3 4 5 6 7 8 9
SCALE OF METRES
1 0 1 2

FIG. 23

5, 23, 24 (pl. VIII B), 26, 28, 43 (later phase) and 108.[1] The *stūpas* inside the *chaitya-gṛihas,* as far as they could be reconstructed, had generally a cylindrical drum surmounted by a low hemisphere – a type reminiscent of the west-Indian caves. Sites 5 and 26 had each two *chaitya-gṛihas*, the former belonged to the Bahuśrutīyas, and comparable with it in many respects was Site 26. Besides the double *chaitya-gṛihas*, both the complexes had within the monastic enclosure chambers externally circular and internally square, It is difficult to be certain, in the absence of any inscription, as to whether Site 26 also belonged to the Bahuśrutīyas. If this affiliation is correct, the presence of a double *chaitya-gṛiha*, each enclosing a *stūpa*, may be taken as a characteristic of this sect at a particular period of its history.[2]

Each of the other sites in this group had only one apsidal temple. Site 24 (pl. VIII B) revealed an inscription of Rudrapurushadatta, the son of Ehuvala Chāṁtamūla and the last known Ikshvāku ruler; it was engraved on a pillar erected in front of the *chaitya-gṛiha* in memory of his mother Vaṁmabhaṭa during his eleventh regnal year.[3] The apsidal shrine at Site 23 was raised within the *vihāra*-enclosure and had a rubble *stūpa* and *āyaka*-platforms. Here the *chaitya-gṛiha* was more conspicuous than the *stūpa* itself. On the basis of the style of the *stūpa*-construction the site may be attributed to some Theravādin sect.

The other monasteries of this group are not much dissimilar to the Aparamahāvina-seliya units. A paved circular structure inside the monastery, the only one of its kind in the valley, was discovered at Site 24. The presence of a *pūrṇa-kumbha* on either side of the entrance to the structure may point to its use as a shrine, though no image was found near by.

C. Unit consisting of stupa, monastery and chaitya-griha with Buddha-image

There are eight monasteries under this group, Sites, 2, 3, 4, 9 (VIII A), 38 (late phase) (IX A), 85, 105 and 106 (pl. XIII). Of them Site 85 had a double shrine for the image, whereas in other cases only one of the two *chaitya-gṛihas* enshrined the Buddha-icon, the other one being meant for a *stūpa*. The *chaitya-gṛihas* of Sites 38, 105 and 106 were later accretions. Site 105 had an oblong chamber with an image of Buddha in the courtyard of the monastery proper. The apsidal structure of Site 106 was possibly added in the twentyfourth year of Ehuvala Chāṁtamūla. The fact that these Buddha-shrines were constructed at a later date may indicate the mounting pressure of some popular opinion, to which the different sects had to give way. The available data show that it was the Aparamahāvina-seliyas who first yielded to this new ideology, being possibly followed by

1 It is difficult to judge from the extant remains whether the *chaitya-gṛiha* of Site 108 was meant for a Buddha-image or a *stūpa,* but in the absence of any icon it has been included provisionally in this group.

2 Ramatirtham, in Visakhapatnam District, also has a double *chaitya-gṛiha* each with a *stūpa*. A third one, also with *stūpa,* is possibly a later addition. As the present condition of the site indicates, the main *stūpa* is without any *āyaka.*

3 *Indian Archaeology 1955-56—A Review* (1956), pp. 23-24.

the Mahāvihāra-vāsins or some other Theravādin sects and the Bahuśrutīyas. So far as epigraphical evidence goes, the earliest monastery having a *chaitya-gṛiha* with Buddha-image is dated in the eighth year of Ehuvala Chāṁtamūla and it was an Apara-mahāvina-seliya monastery (Site 9). Sites 2, 3, 4 and 9 were compact and well-planned units—the *Buddha-chaitya* invariably facing the *stūpa-chaitya*. They were store-houses of beautiful sculptures, executed in bold relief as well as in the round. The sect inhabiting these monasteries perhaps arrived at a reasonable synthesis that attracted the popular imagination and support. It succeeded in assimilating and harmonizing all the prevalent plastic and architectural innovations, thereby transforming the monasteries into galleries of art and architecture. Such establishments were invariably three-winged and had eight spoked *stūpas*. Sculptures herefrom generally portray Buddha in human form, though aniconic ones are also not wanting.

The tide of image-worship that swayed the Nagarjunakonda valley during the reign of Ehuvala Chāṁtamūla reached its zenith when the monastery of Site 85 was renovated. Two shrine-chambers, one apsidal and the other oblong, were constructed, both for installing Buddha. The only other site that had a separate oblong Buddha-shrine was Site 105; that is distinct from the enshrinement of Buddha in an oblong cell attached to the monastery proper in Sites 5, 15, 32 A and 43. It is, therefore, evident that the Buddhists of Nagarjunakonda began without a *chaitya-gṛiha* and the image of Buddha, but eventually the popular urge for the Buddha-icon triumphed over the more orthodox schools of thought and established shrines of Buddha as an indispensable adjunct of a monastery.

D. Unit consisting of monastery and chaitya-griha

There is only one structure under this group, viz. Site 51 (pl. X B), which had no *stūpa*. This may tend to show that unlike most establishments no importance was attached here to the adoration of the *stūpa*.

Site 51 revealed a well-preserved *chaitya-gṛiha* enshrining a *stūpa*, near which was brought to light the extant remains of a monastery, ruthlessly damaged by ploughing. There was no attached *maṇḍapa* or central *stūpa*. Thus, these remains may reveal a line of evolution in a different direction. In Site 23 (above, p. 81) the *chaitya-gṛiha* was given greater prominence than the *stūpa*.

The peculiar complex in Site 78 may be mentioned in this connexion. Here there were at least two apsidal structures placed side by side inside a carved rail (below, p. 88), with two monasteries to the left. A group of subsidiary structures in the shape of oblong, circular, square and octagonal bases existed around the pillared *maṇḍapa* in front of the *chaitya-gṛihas*. One may be inclined to regard these structures as bases of miniature *stūpas*.[1] One of them had clearly a circular outline

[1] The absence of a large *stūpa* at the site has led some to believe that the complex was Brāhmaṇica in character, but the cave-temples of west India are examples where large *stūpas* are absent, the emphasis being on the apsidal shrine with small *stūpas*. However, its location on the river bank where all the Brāhmaṇical shrines were found may tend to prove the Brāhmaṇical character of the site.

on the square pedestal. It is significant to recall that the *stūpas* of north-west India were generally raised on a square platform. Octagonal bases of *stūpas* enshrined in the *chaitya-gṛiha* may also be observed in the Dharmarājikā complex at Taxila.[1] Some of the *stūpas* in the Bagh caves in central India also have octagonal bases.[2]

The earliest apsidal temple of Nagarjunakonda was built by Bodhiśrī in the fourteenth regnal year of Vīrapurushadatta (above, p. 77). Bodhiśrī, it is learnt from an inscription, was also responsible for the construction of another *chaitya-gṛiha* as an adjunct to the Buddhist establishment. Karla, the stronghold of the Mahāsāṅghikas, and other west-Indian caves might have inspired certain architectural devices of Nagarjunakonda. Significantly, the apsidal shrine became common both to the Brāhmaṇical and Buddhist architecture during Ikshvāku rule.

E. Isolated stupas

Five examples of *stūpas*, Sites 15 A, 16 (pl. XI B), 22, 52 and 59 (pl. XIII), possibly *uddeśika* in nature, unconnected with any monastery, etc., have come to light at Nagarjunakonda. All save Site 15 A had *āyaka*-platforms in four directions. Site 16 had the only specimen of a *stūpa* with a ten-spoked base. The *stūpa* of Site 52 was four-spoked on plan, but Site 59 revealed a unique feature in the use of the *svastika* as an inset in the centre of the *stūpa*. Site 15 A had a circular rubble *stūpa* on a hillock without any *āyaka*. The *stūpa* of Site 22 must have had more than one phase. In its earliest form it had a rim made of rubble, the interior being more or less hollow. In the next phase a brick-built rim with projections in four directions was constructed within the diameter of the circular rubble structure. The presence of *āyaka*-platforms in the second phase may help one in identifying it as a *stūpa*, but the core remained unpacked even in this period.

3. THE VOTIVE STUPAS

The inclusion of votive *stūpas* in the monastic establishments of Nagarjunakonda may have some bearing on the changing outlook of the Buddhists residing in the valley. The earliest monasteries did not possess any such *stūpa*, but those of Sites 2, 6, 9, 15, 23, 38, 106, 108 and possibly 26 had them. Out of these eight sites, only two, Sites 9 and 106, yielded datable inscriptions. The *chaitya-gṛiha* of Site 9 was flanked on each of the two sides by a miniature *stūpa*, which, however, did not show any *āyaka*-platform or wheel-shaped base. It may reasonably be surmised that the construction of minor *stūpa* was introduced in the early years of Ehuvala Chāṁtamūla's rule, because Site 9 was renovated in his eighth regnal year. By his twentyfourth year the practice of the construction of minor *stūpas* must have become established, as the monastery of Site 106 built in that year contained as many as eleven votive *stūpas*, four of them arranged at four corners of the main *stūpa*.

[1] John Marshall, *op. cit.*, III, pl. 45.

[2] John Marshall and others (1927), *op, cit.*, pl. 1. Thus, even if it was meant to be a Brāhmaṇical temple it adopted several features from mature Buddhist tradition.

Site 6 yielded four votive *stūpas* of different sizes inside a separate oblong enclosure, one of them with a wheel-base. Site 23 too had four votive *stūpas* inside a similar enclosure. The Mahāvihāra-vāsins accepted this idea at a later date: two votive *stūpas* came into existence during the third structural phase of their monastery in Site 38.

All these votive *stūpas*, with rare exceptions, had a solid core and did not have any *āyaka* platform, save the solitary example of Site 2.

The conception of the votive *stūpa* is intimately connected with the position of the laity in the Buddhist church. There is no doubt that in this period the commoners, including the merchants, promoted the construction of Buddhist buildings to a considerable extent: thus Bodhiśrī, a lay-worshipper, was responsible for many a building, Kumāranandin, a *śreshṭhin*, donated a sculptured frieze in the monastery of Site 106, and the renovation of the second Apara-mahāvina-seliya monastery at Site 9 was effected by gifts received largely from the merchant-community. The fruits expected out of such gifts were '(i) religious merits, for himself, his relatives and friends resulting in their happiness in this world and the next (*ubhaya-loka-hita-sukh-āvahanāya*) and (ii) *nivāṇa-sampati* (*nirvāṇa*-dom) for himself or herself.'[1] This is in consonance with the doctrines of the Chaityaka sect (below, p. 94), which possibly prescribed such gifts to popularize Buddhism amongst the laity. It is but natural that the common people would try to acquire religious merit by donating miniature *stūpas*. During the earlier phase donations were given in the monastery either for its construction or for extensions. But a period must have come when no addition to the existing establishments were feasible or needed, and it was during this period that the idea of donating miniature *stūpas*, which had already assumed wide vogue in Gandhāra (above, p. 56), might have come to stay.

4. THE STUPAS

The majority of the *stūpas* of Nagarjunakonda had wheel-shaped bases with *āyaka*-platforms at the four cardinal directions. These features are generally considered to be typical of the Andhra *stūpa*-architecture. But this is not wholly correct, because Nagarjunakonda disclosed *stūpas* without wheel-bases and *āyaka*-platforms as well, though *stūpas* with these features may be characteristic of a particular sect, perhaps the most dominant one. Practically all the important *stūpas* of Salihundam, District Srikakulam, are without *āyakas*, which are absent at Ramatirtham also.

Most of the *stūpas* of Nagarjunakonda were built of brick, rubble accounting for only six. The *stūpa* of Site 43 had, however, a brick-built rim around an interior packed with rubble and earth. The rubble *stūpas* here were invariably without spokes, but the *stūpas* of Sites 20, 23 and 28 had *āyaka*-platforms. A rubble *stūpa* with a wheel-base is noticed in the large *stūpa* at Kodavali, District East Godavari; it is built on a terraced platform with a solid hub and two concentric circles.

The introduction of a wheel-shaped plan for the larger *stūpas* was motivated

[1] Dutt, *op. cit.*, p. 106.

mainly by considerations of structural stability and economy of material. A small *stūpa* of either brick or rubble does not require so much attention so far as stability and economy are concerned. There is also a possibility that this developed constructional feature might have drawn its inspiration from the *dharma-chakra* symbol. Hence, in wheel-shaped *stūpas* one may not only notice an improvement over an earlier building-tradition but also a successful attempt at transforming an idea, a symbol, into an architectural entity. It is difficult to assign the credit of this innovation to any particular sect. The fact that the Chaityakas formed a distinct school of their own in Āndhra-deśa[1] may faintly suggest that they possibly specialized in this developed mode of *stūpa*-construction (below, p. 88).

That ideology sometimes influenced the form of the *stūpa* is also evident from the *stūpas* with *svastika*-inset in the centre. Nagarjunakonda had three such examples, viz. the *stūpas* of Site 20 (pl. XII A), 59 (pl. XIII) and possibly 108. These *svastikas*, being in the centre of the base, were obviously not visible from outside. Since such an arrangement cannot have any architectural significance it may definitely be said that they were due to some ideological consideration. The only other *stūpa* outside Nagarjunakonda reported to have a *svastika* symbol was at Peddaganjam, District Guntur,[2] where the largest *stūpa* had a number of bricks in the form of a *svastika*. That Buddha is shown in the form of a *svastika* may easily be gathered from the sculptural representations of Amaravati and Nagarjunakonda. Thus considered, the wheel-shaped plan also might have been motivated by some ideological concept harmonized with architectural requirements. But it will also be apparent from the following discussions that the number of spokes in a *stūpa* was generally connected with its size.

The earliest *stūpa* at Nagarjunakonda, Site 1, was, as already stated (above, p. 76), wheel-shaped on plan. There were eight examples of eight-spoked, six of four-spoked, two of six-spoked and one of ten-spoked *stūpas*. The first circle of the *stūpas* of Sites 5 and 9 had eight spokes, but the number of cross-walls connecting this with the outer concentric circle was twelve and sixteen respectively. On the basis of diameter the *stūpas* may be divided into six groups, viz., (i) below 20 ft. (6·1 m.), (ii) between 20 (6·1 m.) and 30 ft. (9·1 m.), (iii) between 30 (9·1 m.) and 40 ft. (12·2 m.), (iv) between 40 (12·2 m.) and 50 ft. (15·2 m.), (v) between 50 (15·2 m.) and 60 ft. (18·3 m.) and (vi) 91 ft. (27·7 m.). The first group is represented by seven examples—Sites 15, 15 A, 27, 38, 59, 86 and 108—of which two definitely belonged to the four-spoked variety; of the rest, one had *svastika*-inset and the other four were without spokes. The maximum concentration is in group (ii), represented by thirteen examples—Sites 4, 14, 22, 23, 26, 30, 32, 32 A, 32 B, 43, 52, 54 and 105. Only two *stūpas*—Sites 4 and 26—in this group had eight spokes; all the four four-spoked and two six-spoked ones, besides, five spokeless rubble *stūpas* belong to this diameter-group. Eight *stūpas*—Sites 2, 3, 7, 8, 20, 24, 85 and 106, six of them being eight-spoked, may be included in group (iii). Only three *stūpas*—Sites 5, 9 and 16—fall in

[1] The Chaityakas were so called on account of their devotion to the *chaitya*. Dutt, *op. cit.*, p. 51.

[2] A. Rea, *South Indian Buddhist Antiquities* (Madras, 1894), p. 3. See, however, below, p. 90, n. 2

group (iv). There are two examples—Sites 6 and 21—in group (v) and the last group is represented by a solitary *stūpa*—Site 1.

The position is summarized in the sub-joined table.

TABLE IV

Table showing the relation of diameters of stūpa with the number of spokes

Number of spokes	Site	Range of diameter
Four	14	20 to 30 ft. (6·1 m. to 9·1 m.)
	27	,, ,,
	52	,, ,,
	54	,, ,,
	105	,, ,,
	108	,, ,,
Six	30	20 to 30 ft. (6·1 m. to 9·1 m.)
	32 A	,, ,,
Eight	4	20 to 30 ft. (6·1 m. to 9·1 m.)
	26	,, ,,
	2	30 to 40 ft. (9·1 m. to 12·2 m)
	3	,, ,,
	7	,, ,,
	24	,, ,,
	85	,, ,,
	106	,, ,,
	6	50 to 60 ft. (15·2 m. to 18·3 m.)
	21	,, ,,
Ten	16	40 to 50 ft. (12·2 m. to 15·2 m.)
Eight in the inner circle and twelve in the outer ...	5	40 to 50 ft. (12·2 m. to 15·2 m.)
Eight in the inner circle and sixteen in the outer ...	9	40 to 50 ft. (12·2 m. to 15·2 m.)
Eight in the innermost circle and sixteen each in the central and outermost ...	1	91 ft. (27·7 m.)

It will be seen from the Table IV that four-spoked *stūpas* conform to three different diameters, viz. 27 ft. or 8·2 m. (Site 14), 22 ft. or 6·7 m. (Sites 52, 54, and 105) and 15 ft. or 4·6 m. (Sites 27 and 108). Hence, it may safely be concluded that no four-spoked *stūpa* had a diameter of more than 28 ft. (8·5 m.). The width of the *āyaka*-platform in these *stūpas* varied between 1 ft. 6 in. (0·45 m.) to 1 ft. 11 in. (0·58 m.). This narrow width could hardly provide space for *āyaka*-pillars. One peculiar feature of the four-spoked *stūpas* is the general absence of the Buddha-shrine in the establishments containing them. The *stūpas* of Sites 27 and 108 did not show any *āyaka*-platform; furthermore, no hub could be seen in the centre, whereas in all other cases it was either square or circular in form.

Two six-spoked *stūpas*, Sites 30 (pl. XI A) and 32 A, situated close to each other, had diameters of 27 and 28 ft. (8·5 m.). The *āyakas* of Site 30 may be termed as incipient platforms. The other one, Site 32 A, had *āyaka*-platforms, measuring 6 ft. (1·8 m) x 1 ft. 2 in. (0·35 m.). It is unlikely that any pillar could have been installed on a platform with such a narrow width. Site 30 was without any *maṇḍapa* or *chaitya-gṛiha*. On the other hand, Site 32 A revealed a Buddha-*chaitya* oblong in shape, probably a later addition. As the monastery of Site 30 had only three cells, a guess may be hazarded that it was the monastery of dissenters who separated themselves from the original monastery of Site 32 A. If that is correct, the six-spoked *stūpas* would stand as a symbol of common inheritance. At the same time, it is worth noting that none of the four or six-spoked *stūpas* had a diameter of more than 28 ft. (8·5 m.).

Eight-spoked *stūpas* were ten in number, excluding Sites 5 and 9, both having double concentric circles. The *stūpa* of Site 5 had two concentric rings of eight and twelve spokes, respectively with diameters of 24 ft. (7·3 m.) and 49 ft. (15 m.), besides a hub, 4 ft. 4 in. (1·32 m.) square. The core of the *stūpa* was divided into twenty chambers, eight in the inner and twelve in the outer rings. The *stūpa* in Site 9 as well had two concentric circles with 24 ft. (7·3 m.) and 41 ft. 9 in. (12·7 m.) diameters and with eight and sixteen spokes respectively. But the builders of the *stūpas* of Sites 6 and 21, each with a diameter of more than 50 ft. (15·2 m.), did not feel the necessity of having more than one circle, which may imply that the outer rings of the *stūpas* of Sites 5 and 9 were afterthoughts.

It is apparent from the above that the number of spokes in a *stūpa* was largely subservient to its dimensions. *Stūpas* having more than 28 ft. (8·5 m.) diameter had invariably eight spokes. Conversely, those of less than 28 ft. (8·5 m.) in diameter generally had either four or six spokes. The numbers of spokes had thus a constructional utility. At the same time, as stated above (p. 85), the possibility of the numbers being symbolic representations of particular episodes of Buddha's life or of aspects of his teachings may not altogether be ruled out. This possibility is apparent in the ten-spoked *stūpa* of Site 16, measuring 47 ft. 3 in. (14·4 m.) in diameter, with a solid circular hub of as large as 12 ft. 6 in. (3·8 m.) in diameter; a *stūpa* of such dimensions could easily have been constructed on eight spokes, such as the larger *stūpas* of Sites 6 and 21. Similarly, from the structural point of view, four spokes would have sufficed in those *stūpas* which have six.

A few miscellaneous facts about the *stūpas* and on the occurrence of railing may be noted here. There is not a single six, eight or ten-spoked *stūpa* without *āyaka*-platforms, though the platforms might not always have carried *āyaka*-pillars. Only those without spokes and a few four-spoked ones did not have any platforms. *Stūpas* carved on the drum-slabs often display railings around them. In all probability, the *stūpa* of Site 1 had a circular railing. Longhurst thinks that 'the railings and gateways were of carved wood and stone on brick foundation. It was only on very rare occasions that they were executed in stone.'[1] Yet so far no evidence of wooden rail is available at Nagarjunakonda: on the other hand, the Reserve Collection of the Site Museum there contains no less than thirty pieces of plain limestone cross-bars of an identical type. They have a plano-convex cross-section, and are without any well-defined tenon; in length they vary from 15½″ to 13½″ (0·4 to 0·3 m.). Unfortunately their provenance is not known, nor are the corresponding types of copings and uprights available. In the same collection are also found a few uprights carved with lotus medallion, besides some decorated cross-bars, with lenticular cross-section—sculptural embellishment on the cross-bars, as now available, comprising boldly-executed figure of elephant-within-medallion. In all likelihood these pieces came from Site 3, and might have been the remains of an oblong rail, brick foundation of which was extant at the time of the excavation. Site 78 (above, p. 82) too had an oblong rail around the apsidal shrines; the rail, elegantly carved with variety of sculptures executed in bold relief, consisted of several monolithic parts, each forming a complete piece of a highly sophisticated limestone railing of a low height. It is equally true that many *stūpas* were definitely without railings. Some *stūpas* were built on high square platforms; at least half-a-dozen stood on hillocks.[2] Needless to say, some *stūpas* were highly decorated, the decoration extending over the full length of the hemisphere; the drum-portion was generally encased with sculptured slabs.

Both the *stūpas* of the Theravādin sects, Site 38 and 43, were small in size. Possibly they did not put so much emphasis on the main *stūpa* as the Apara-mahāvina-seliyas, Bahuśrutīyas and Mahīśāsakas. Despite the fact that Sites 6, 20 and 21 were without any *maṇḍapa* and apsidal temple, the *stūpas* here were of large dimensions. This prominence given to the *stūpa* may be, as already hinted (above, p. 85), a characteristic of the Apara-mahavina-seliyas or the Chaityakas.

***Stūpas* with wheel-shaped plan appear to belong to an evolved stage of *stūpa*-architecture. The *stūpa* of Amaravati had a solid core like that of Sanchi. Even the gigantic *stūpa* at Bhattiprolu, of the second century B.C., approximates the solid variety, though its central portion is wheel-shaped; here one sees the beginnings of this style in Āndhra-deśa. But the *stūpa* at Piprahwa had almost an identical feature too. It is, however, difficult to say if the *stūpas* of Bhattiprolu (fig. 24) and Piprahwa were precursors of actual wheel-shaped plan. Incidentally, dates of both the aforesaid**

1 Longhurst, *op. cit.*, p. 13.

2 It is curious, however, that no establishment of the Apara-mahāvina-seliyas was erected on a hill in spite of the name of the sect being associated with *śaila* ('hill').

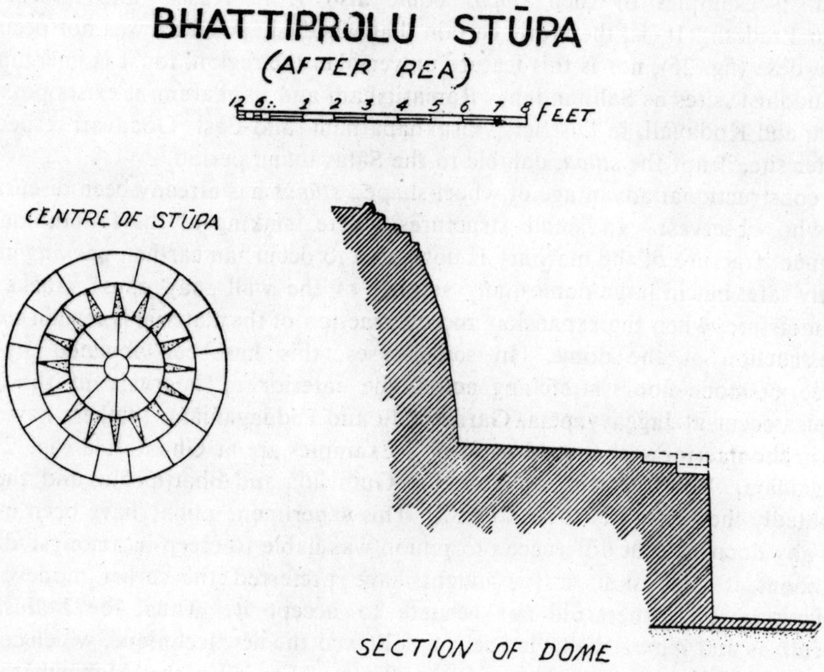

FIG. 24

stūpas are not based on firm stratigraphic data, nor one can say emphatically that the *stūpas* in their present form were coeval with the dates of the inscribed relic caskets recovered from the respective sites. Let it be mentioned here that the wheel-shaped plan is not confined to Āndhra-deśa only for a phase of the Dharmarājikā *stūpa* at Taxila and the one from Sirkap (above, p. 64) were irregularly wheel-shaped on plan; also wheel-shaped were the *stūpas* at Mathurā (above, p. 19) and Shāh-ji-Dheri at Peshawar.[1] Undoubtedly, the *stūpas* with wheel-shaped plan at Taxila and Mathurā were chronologically anterior to even the earliest *stūpa* at Nagarjunakonda. Also significant is their early occurrence in the territory of the foreign rulers. Does it mean that this type of specialized construction was introduced here by the Śaka-Parthians? No definite answer to this question can be given unless the dates of the Bhattiprolu and Piprahwa are firmly fixed. Further, in close proximity to the main *stūpa* at the last-mentioned site was found, as the plan of the site shows, a small *stūpa*, described in the Report as a well, which appears to be the remains of a spoked *stūpa*;[2] its date is also not known. A *stūpa* at Barā-Pahārī near Patna had wheel-like arrangement of

[1] *An. Rep. Arch. Surv. Ind.*, 1908-09 (1912), p. 48.

[2] Purna Chandra Mukherjee, *A Report on a tour of exploration of the Antiquities in the Tarai, Nepal* (Calcutta, 1901), pl. XXVII.

the walls;[1] examples of such *stūpas* come also from Kasia[2] and Ahichchhatra in Uttar Pradesh. It is, therefore, certain that wheel-shaped plan was not peculiar to Āndhra-deśa (fig. 26), nor is this feature universal in the region, for it is uncommon at such Buddhist sites as Salihundam, Ramatirtham and Sankaram; it exists possibly at Kotturu and Kodavali, in Districts Visakhapatnam and East Godavari respectively, the latter site, if not the *stūpa*, datable to the Sātavāhana period.

The constructional advantage of wheel-shaped *stūpas* has already been discussed by Rea, who observes: 'In small structures where sinking of the foundations, and consequent fracture of the masonry is not liable to occur, an earthen packing may be perfectly safe; but in large domes, any sinking of the wall may cause cracks which admit moisture, when the expansion and contraction of the material is certain to cause the destruction of the dome. In some cases, this has been obviated by brick, concrete, or stone floors stretching across the interior at intervals in the height. Examples occur at Jaggayyapēṭa, Garikapāḍu and Peddagañjām. Others have cross-walls in the interior with a mud-packing. Examples are at Ghaṇtaśālā (fig. 25) and Peddagañjām. Solid domes are found at Guḍivāḍā and Bhaṭṭiprōḷu; and these are undoubtedly the earliest of these *stūpas*.' This experiment might have been irrespective of any doctrine, but difference of opinion was liable to creep in amongst different sects about its adoption; a few might have preferred the earlier mode of solid construction, while others did not hesitate to accept it. Thus, the Mahīśāsakas, Bahuśrutīyas and Apara-mahāvina-seliyas followed the new technique, which could be given a doctrinal colour by them. Some Theravādins like the Mahāvihāra-vāsins refused to make any concession, though some groups within the Theravādins might have kept pace with the times by adopting this new architectural feature.

Even the *āyaka*-platforms are not peculiar to Āndhra-deśa (fig. 26). The recent excavation at Vaiśālī[3] has brought to light remains of a *stūpa* with such platforms. Though a projection, somewhat similar to the *āyaka*, is found on only one side of the *stūpa* hewn out of a rock at Sankaram,[4] it is not noticed at sites like Ramatirtham[5] and Salihundam. The fact that the *stūpas* with wheel-base and with *āyaka*-platforms are discovered at or near Vaiśālī may vaguely be ascribed to the spread of the Mahāsāṅghikas (also, p. 12), who had their original stronghold at Vaiśālī and from whose doctrines the Śailas (including the Apara-mahāvina-seliyas) derived theirs.[6]

5. THE MONASTERIES

At the initial stages the residential part of an establishment at Nagarjunakonda formed an independent unit, though situated close to the corresponding place

1 *An. Rep. Arch. Surv. Ind., Eastern Circle, for* 1915-16 (Calcutta, 1916), p. 32. Information from Shri A. Ghosh.

2 The Nirvāṇa *stūpa* of Kasia (Kuśīnagara) may have had a *svastika* in the core, though the available report may refer to a four-spoked wheel, *An. Rep. Arch. Surv. Ind.*, 1910-11 (1914), p. 64.

3 *Indian Archaeology 1957-58—A Review* (1958), p. 10 and pl. VIII B.

4 *An. Rep. Arch. Surv. Ind.*, 1908-09, pls. LXII and LXIII.

5 Ibid., 1910-11, pl. XL.

6 Nalinaksha Dutt, *op. cit.*, (1930), pp. 21-22.

of worship. For example, at Site 1 the *mahāvihāra* was quite distinct from the *mahā-chaitya* and the adjoining *chaitya-gṛiha*. Sites 6, 20, 21, 27, 28, 30 etc. had the main *stūpa* at some distance from the *vihāra*, the whole-complex being surrounded by a compound-wall. Even at Sites 5, 7-8, 9, 15, 24, 26, 43, 54, 105 and 106 the residential portion was separated from the *stūpa* or *chaitya-gṛiha*. Such an arrangement may suggest the division of each establishment into two main components, viz., portions accessible and not accessible to the commoners. *Chaitya-gṛihas* were, at the beginning, situated in the area accessible to the public, but subsequently they became part and parcel of the residential area, the typical examples being Sites 2, 3, 4, 23, 85 and 105. Obviously, the worship of the *stūpa* or the image

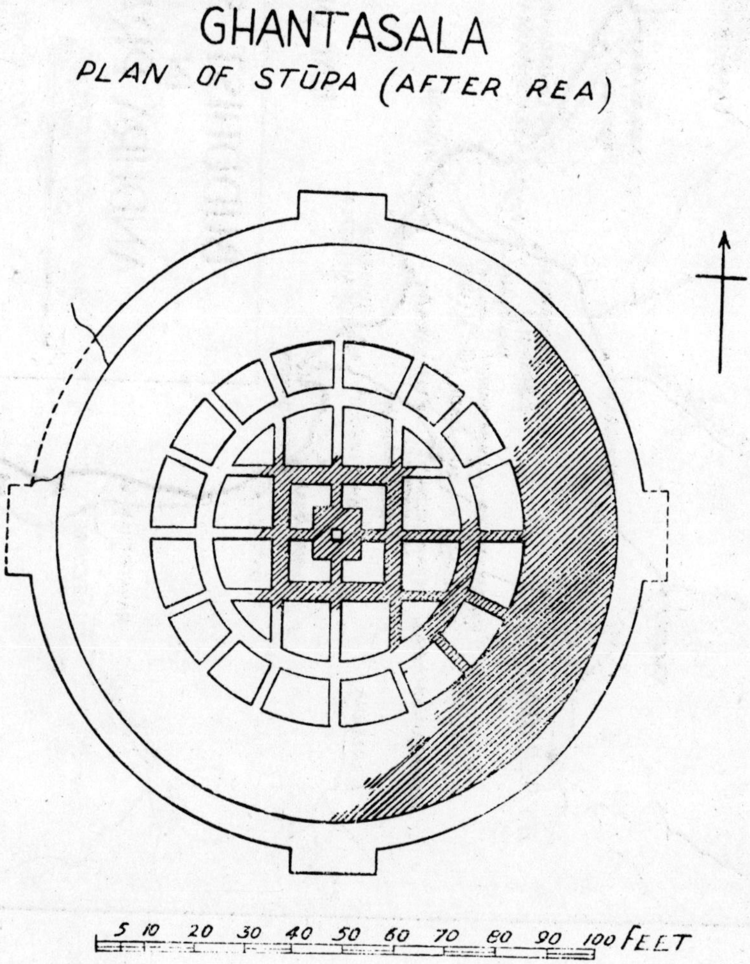

FIG. 25

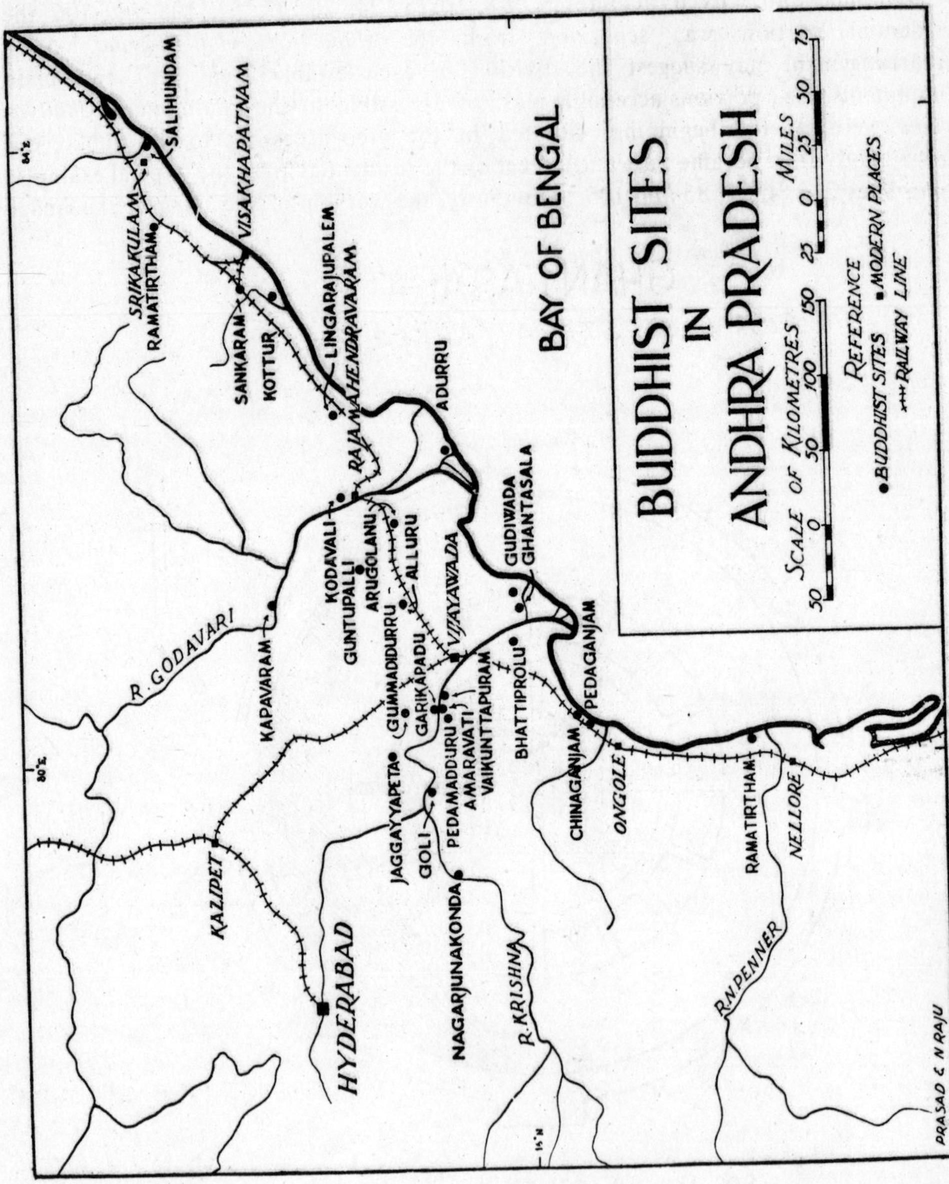
BUDDHIST SITES
IN
ANDHRA PRADESH
BAY OF BENGAL
SCALE OF KILOMETRES
50 0 50 100 150
MILES
25 0 25 50 75
REFERENCE
BUDDHIST SITES
MODERN PLACES
RAILWAY LINE
SRIKAKULAM
SALIHUNDAM
RAMATIRTHAM
VISAKHAPATNAM
LINGARAJUPALEM
SANKARAM
KOTTUR
RAJAMAHENDRAVARAM
ADURRU
KODAVALI
GUNTUPALLI
ARUGOLANU
ALLURU
VIJAYAWADA
GUDIWADA
GHANTASALA
R. GODAVARI
KAPAVARAM
GUMMADIDURRU
GARIKAPADU
AMARAVATI
VAIKUNTTAPURAM
BHATTIPROLU
PEDAGANJAM
CHINAGANJAM
ONGOLE
RAMATIRTHAM
NELLORE
JAGGAYYAPETA
GOLI
PEDAMADDURU
NAGARJUNAKONDA
KAZIPET
HYDERABAD
R. KRISHNA
R.N. PENNER
PRASAD & N RAJU

FIG. 26

of Buddha inside *chaitya-gṛiha* was given more importance in the tenets of certain sects than the *stūpa* proper, which, with its gradually-diminishing size, possibly became only the object of veneration primarily of the lay-worshipper. When the Bahuśrutīyas started worship of Buddha, the shrines were constructed within the residential part. Site 38, belonging to the Mahāvihāra-vāsins, was an exception in all respects, because whereas at other sites the *stūpa* stood in an area accessible to all, at this site even the *stūpa*, not to speak of *chaitya-gṛiha*, was surrounded by a four-winged *vihāra*. Such variations in the general lay-out are difficult to explain but would obviously reflect a particular type of attitude. It is well-known that the Theravādins at first were not in favour of giving the laity a prominent place in their scheme.

The Bahuśrutīya monastery, Site 5, was one of the largest at Nagarjunakonda, so far as the number of cells is concerned. It had at least twentyeight cells, besides an oblong Buddha-shrine and three special chambers, two of which were circular externally and square internally and the third oblong. These chambers might have been meant for the *āchārya*, *vinaya-dhara*, etc. who might have preferred to have separate cells of their own. But this was, again, a new development, since the *mahāvihāra* of Site 1 did not have any such chamber. Even the Mahīśāsaka and Mahāvihāra-vāsin monasteries, Sites 7-8 and 38, have more or less uniform cells. Site 26, almost identical on plan with Bahuśrutīya, also possessed two such special chambers. The number of such rooms at Site 32 A was three and all of them had stone benches, thereby suggesting their use as residential cells. It is, therefore, fairly certain that leading monks of certain sects maintained some aloofness from the rest.

The number of monastic cells varied from two to thirty or even more.[1] Site 86 had two cells and was the smallest unit. Sites 27 and 30 had each three cells and Site 108 five. As already stated (above, p. 87), Sites 27 and 108 each had four-spoked *stūpas* without *āyaka*-platforms and Site 30 a six-spoked one. These small units may be the monasteries of the schismatics. Site 108 would exhibit certain features very similar to Site 38, whereas Sites 27 and 30 might have belonged to the dissident groups of Sites 32 B and 32 A respectively, though this is only a conjecture. There were monasteries with arrangement for the accommodation variously of nine, ten, twelve, thirteen, fifteen, sixteen, nineteen, twenty, twentyone and twentytwo persons. The *mahāvihāra* of Site 1 had at least twentyfive cells and, as stated above, the Bahuśrutīya monastery, Site 5, had twentyeight normal cells. The largest unit was Site 32 A, to provide room for 30 persons. Approximately, the size of the monastic population of Nagarjunakonda, which naturally might have included temporary inhabitants, was about four hundred and fifty. The size of the individual cells varied

[1] According to the *Mahāvagga*, IX, 4, 1, Sacred Books of the East, XVII (1882), p. 268, there are five kinds of *saṅghas*, variously consisting of four, five, ten, twenty and more than twenty persons. According to the *Chullavagga*, VII, 5, 1-2, *ibid.*, XX (1885), pp. 265-67, nine dissenters are sufficient to create a schism (*saṅgha-bheda*) and thereafter they may perform their rituals independently; four dissenters can cause a dissension (*saṅgha-rāji*).

from 7 to 9 ft. (2·1 to 2·7 m.). The developed units, e.g. Sites 3 and 4, had refectories, store-rooms, etc., attached to the monasteries.

A *maṇḍapa* or the congregational hall was absent at Sites 2, 20, 21, 27, 30, 37, 38 and 105; what this absence actually means is not easy to surmise. Though the western half of Site 32 A is generally said to have been a nunnery, the evidence is not definite; in fact, it is not possible to identify any nunnery, even though the testimony of inscriptions may suggest the presence of nuns at Nagarjunakonda.

6. CONCLUSION

The history of the monastic development at Nagarjunakonda thus discloses a complicated picture. The first wave of Buddhism that reached the valley was, broadly speaking, a mixed Hīnayāna Buddhism, to use Dutt's terminology.[1] The earliest *mahā-chaitya* was that of the Apara-mahāvina-seliyas, built in the sixth regnal year of Vīrapurushadatta. There is evidence to prove that the worship of the Buddha-image was not originally in their tenets; nor did they favour the construction of the apsidal temple. Possibly they did not even approve the idea of representing Buddha in human form. Like the Chaityakas or Lokottaravādins they gave special prominence to the worship of the *chaitya* (*stūpa*): one could acquire merit by the erection, decoration and circumambulation of the *chaitya* and by offerings of flowers, garlands, etc., to it. The path for acquiring piety was not complicated, and one may detect in such doctrines the urge of the sects to bring into their folds as many adherents as possible. The Lokottaravādin trends, in some form or the other, were pursued by the majority of the sects of Nagarjunakonda. Some of the Theravādin sects were, however, an exception, as their *stūpas* did not attain any great distinction: nor did they construct *stūpas* with *ayaka*-platforms. There is a possibility that a few of these sects were even against the idea of the wheel-shaped *stūpa*. But the Mahīśāsaka Theravādins, who were the only sect which preferred the double *stūpa* to the *chaitya-gṛiha*, gave more importance to the *stūpa* than even the Apara-mahāvina-seliyas and the Bahusrutīyas. By far the largest number of Buddhists adhered to the original Apara-mahāvina-seliya type of establishments similar to Site 1 (early phase), comprising the *stūpa* proper and residential cells. The *Mahāvastu*, the *vinaya* of the Lokottaravādins, portrays somewhat a similar picture of an age when the Lokottara conception of Buddha had not yet taken hold on the people's mind: Buddha had already been deified but was not represented in anthropomorphic form.[2] In all likelihood, the Lokottaravādins, at least in the beginning of their career, had a predisposition for symbolic representation of Buddha. The Apara-mahāvina-seliyas introduced almost an identical tradition at Nagarjunakonda.

A study of sculptures from the different sites should normally throw light on this aspect of development, but the chronological sequence of the earlier collection in the local Museum has not been studied. It appears to the present writer that some sites,

1 Dutt, *op. cit.* (1930), p. 4.
2 Dutt, *op. cit.*, (1930), p. 25, and (1945), pp 293-98.

such as Sites 1 and 6, had practically no piece where Buddha was shown in human form. There is only one drum-slab with Buddha-figure in the Museum which is recorded to have been picked up from Site 6, but the style of its execution is different from that of other examples from the same site. In this slab the Bodhi-tree is depicted behind the scene of Buddha's First Sermon in the Deer park, but this motif appears to be the characteristic of the sculptures from the *stūpas* of Sites 2 and 3. Sculptures from Site 1 exhibit only symbolic representations of Buddha. Thus, the authors of Sites 1 and 6 did not possibly favour the carving of Buddha in anthropomorphic form. Let it be emphasized here that the symbolic representation does not necessarily imply a high antiquity, for it might have been inherent in the faith of a particular sect.

That some section of the Apara-mahāvina-seliyas acceded to the idea of image-worship during the eighth regnal year of Ehuvala Chāṁtamūla is evident from a mutilated Buddha-image from a *chaitya-gṛiha* of Site 9, belonging to that year. The Mahāvihāra-vāsins, and the Bahuśrutīyas also followed suit (above, p. 78). Sects inhabiting Sites 2, 3, 4 and 106, which yielded the best specimens of sculptures,[1] were also believers in image-worship. They often represent Buddha in human form, and each site had a *chaitya-gṛiha* meant for the icon. The Mahīśāsakas, like the original Apara-mahāvina-seliyas, did not yield to the popular demand of image-worship. A stage, however, came in the development of Buddhist establishments at Nagarjunakonda when both the *chaitya-gṛihas* (Site 85) were adorned with images, neither of them being reserved for a *stūpa*.

During the period of idolization, *stūpas* were possibly relegated to the background and at some sites the apsidal shrine became the most imposing edifice. In other words the temple-concept gained greater currency. During the latter part of the rule of Vīrapurushadatta both the Theravādins as well as the Apara-mahāvina-seliyas allowed *chaitya-gṛihas* to come up. It was possibly Bodhiśrī, the lay-worshipper from Govagrāma, who introduced the *chaitya-gṛiha* at Nagarjunakonda (above, p. 83). At that time this conception might not have had any far-reaching effect on the prevailing doctrines of the different sects. At the next stage, controversy as to the relative importance of the *chaitya-gṛiha* and the main *stūpa* might have arisen. Subsequently, *chaitya-gṛihas* were raised within the precincts of the residential enclosure. Thus, the emphasis was transferred from the *stūpa* to the shrine.

[1] On the basis of the datable specimens the sculptural art of Nagarjunakonda may broadly be divided into two phases. The early phase, coinciding with the rule of Vīrapurushadatta, produced sculptures characterized by low relief, rigid lines and some amount of stylization in the delineation of various motifs. All the masterpieces of the Ikshvāku art came from the developed phase which reached its heights in the latter years of Ehuvala Chāṁtamūla. Executed in bold relief these sculptures are known for rhythm and clarity of lines, distributed balance, vivid portryal of human moods, superior story-element and, above all, in their spontaneous appeal. The developed phase started some time in the eighth regnal year of Ehuvala. See H. Sarkar and B.N. Mishra, *op. cit.*, pp. 45-51.

The image-worship and the concomitant apsidal and, later on, square or oblong shrines were steps towards further popularization of Buddhism. The creed and ideology of different sects except the Mahīśāsakas and the original Apara-mahāvina-seliyas, who stood firm against the tide, had to undergo metamorphosis in order to make room for these changes, which were the general trend of the time. Such changes reflected themselves in the monastic set-up and plastic art as well.

CHAPTER SIX

SECTS AND ARCHAEOLOGICAL EVIDENCE

Neither the archaeological evidence nor any literary source can tell when exactly the ideological difference or differences in the *vinaya* rules led to the formation of various sects. That some discontent was already there amongst the followers of Gautama Buddha even during his life-time is evident not only from the story of the quarrel between the two teachers at Kauśāmbī[1] but also from Devadatta's episode.[2] Significant also are the remarks made by Subhadra immediately after the *parinirvāṇa*: 'Enough, brethern! Weep not, neither lament! We are well rid of the great Samana. We used to be annoyed by being told, "This beseems you, this beseems you not." But now we shall be able to do whatever we like; and what we do not like, that we shall not have to do!'[3] Moreover, the role of the Chhabbaggia (Shaḍvargika) *bhikshus* in the *Vinaya* texts as if constantly violating the rules of discipline may also suggest that certain disruptive tendencies were at work inside the Buddhist *saṅgha* either during Buddha's life-time or in the period when the *Vinaya* was being compiled. Also the very necessity of holding the First Buddhist Council at Rājagṛiha bespeaks the presence of factional elements amongst the followers of Buddha, and the fact that Mahākassapa failed to secure Gavampati and Purāṇa's approval of the texts settled by his Council[4] also suggests growing dissensions amongst the veteran monks.

Despite these discontents or differences of opinion the *saṅgha* did not possibly witness total schism until the Second Buddhist Council, which was held at Vaiśālī perhaps during the rule of Kālāśoka of the Pali tradition.[5] This Council saw a total cleavage of the *saṅgha* into orthodox school and the Mahāsāṅghikas—the latter included some

1 N. Dutt, *Early Monastic Buddhism*, II (Calcutta, 1945), p. 6.

2 *Ibid.*, pp. 6-7. Hiuen Tsang refers to the existence of the followers of Devadatta at Karṇasuvarṇa as late as the seventh century. He writes, 'There were also three Buddhist monasteries in which in accordance with the teaching of Devadatta milk products were not taken as food.' See Thomas Watters, *On Yuan Chwang's Travels in India* (A.D. 629-645) (Delhi, 1961), p. 191.

3 *Chullavagga*, Sacred Books of the East, XX (1885), p. 371.

4 N. Dutt (1945), *op. cit.*, pp. 10-11, writes 'In the proceedings of the First Council it will be observed that Mahākassapa was keen on securing the approval of all the senior monks, particularly, of Gavampati and Purāṇa, of the texts settled by his Council as *Buddhavacana*. Gavampati remained neutral, i e. he did not wholeheartedly accept the proceedings of the Council as final while Purāṇa expressed his inability to accept the same as the words of the Teacher. He further insisted on the incorporation into the *Vinaya* of eight rules relating to food.'

5 Some scholars like D. R. Bhandarkar, R. K. Mookerji, B. G. Gokhale etc. have suggested that the Second Council 'really came off in the reign of Aśoka and not earlier as claimed by the Ceylon chronicles.' See B. G. Gokhale, *Buddhism and Asoka* (Baroda, 1948), p. 78.

of the monks from Vaiśālī who, after separating themselves, held a larger convention known as Mahāsaṅgha or Mahāsaṅgīti. Organized primarily by Yasa of Kauśāmbī the Second Council made an attempt to settle the question of ten unlawful rules[1] followed by the Vajjian monks of Vaiśālī, who, as it were, represented the Easterners as opposed to the other group of monks hailing mostly from western regions like Mathurā, Avantī and Kauśāmbī. Perhaps geographical division later manifested itself in ideological sphere too, for the Mahāsāṅghikas with their centre around Pāṭaliputra formed a distinct sect with their rivals Theravādins and the Sarvāstivādins holding their positions respectively at Kauśāmbī and Mathurā.[2]

The division of the Buddhist *saṅgha* did not, however, find its expression in Aśoka's edicts which presumed more or less a unified *saṅgha* throughout. The mention of *saṅghe samage kaṭe* (the *saṅgha* is made whole and entire) in Sanchi and Kauśāmbī pillar-inscriptions[3] reflects some sort of unification, if not averting of a schism, of the two drifting branches under the stewardship of the emperor Aśoka. A stern attitude on his part to curb all disruptive tendencies throughout the country manifests itself also in the very fact of the promulgation of the schism-edicts. His directives to officers, as contained in the Sanchi and Kauśāmbī pillar-inscriptions,[4] to quash all rifts in the *saṅgha*, his recommendation in the Bairat edict[5] of certain texts for special study of the monks, and the declaration that the *saṅgha* was made one and that he wanted concord in the Buddhist church clearly show his concern and active interference in matters of Buddhist *saṅgha*. His inscription also records that the dissenting monks and nuns should be ostracized after making them wear white robes.[6] He possibly went to such an extent as to behead the 'unorthodox' monks; both the Pali as well as the Sanskrit traditions, though varying in details with one another, are more or less unanimous on this point.[7]

The Third Buddhist Council, the account of which did not find any mention in the Sanskrit, Chinese and Tibetan sources, is said to have taken place at Pāṭaliputra during Aśoka's time. Its mention in the Ceylonese chronicles has led scholars to believe that 'it was a sectarian affair, for which it was ignored by all sects except the Theravādins, to be more precise, Theravāda-Vibhajjavāda sect of Ceylon.'[8] Judging in the light of Aśoka's edicts, the Council, whatever may be its aim and outcome, was not perhaps purely sectarian, for Aśoka fought for unity in the *saṅgha*. At the same

[1] For details, see N. Dutt (1945), *op. cit.*, pp. 35-36.

[2] N. Dutt (1945), *op. cit.*, pp. 29-30.

[3] E. Hultzsch, *Corpus Inscriptionum Indicarum*, I (Inscriptions of Aśoka), pp. 158-160.

[4] *Ibid*, p. 159. *Ye saṁghaṁ bhākhati bhikhu vā bhikhuni vā odātāni dusāni sanaṁdhāpayitu anāvāsasi vāsāpetaviye.*

[5] *Ibid*, p. 172. The following texts have been recommended (i) *the Vinaya-samukasa,* (ii) *the Aliya-vasas,* (iii) the *Anāgata-bhayas,* (iv) the *Muni-gāthās,* (v) the *Moneya-sūta,* (vi) the *Upatisa-pasina*, and (vii) the *Lāghulo-vāda.*

[6] Hultzsch, *op. cit.*, p. 159. Also, above n. 4.

[7] N. Dutt, *op. cit.*, (1945), pp. 251-52.

[8] N. Dutt, *ibid.*, pp. 265-70. Also, Kern, *Manual of Buddhism*, p. 11. For views of other scholars, see B. G. Gokhale, *op. cit.*, 77-78.

time, the role that Aśoka played in the propagation of the religion by imparting novel ideas including the concept of shrine, should have invited criticism from the orthodox section. But the Theravāda tradition did not hesitate to announce loudly its association with Aśoka, and what is more, neither Moggaliputta Tissa nor Yonaka Dhammarakkhita, the *Saṅghatthera* of Pāṭaliputra[1] raised any voice against the new architectural, and concomitantly, gradual ideological changes. Thus, if the story of Aśoka's connexion with the Theravādins is true one may as well assume that some section of this sect supported not only the *stūpa*-cult but also the idea of shrine as early as the third century B.C.

Mogaliputta Tissa by virtue of his association with Aśoka possibly got an opportunity to spread Theravāda doctrines to different parts of India and Ceylon, and nine missionaries were sent to nine different places e.g., Kāśmira-Gandhāra, Mahishamaṇḍala, Vanavāsi, Aparānta, Mahāraṭṭha, Yona countries, Himavanta, Suvaṇṇabhūmi and Tambapaṇṇi (*Mahāvaṁsa*, ch. XII). The absence of Āndhra region in the list is likely to suggest the presence of the Mahāsāṅghikas there; similarly, the spread of the Theravāda doctrine did not perhaps affect Mathurā which remained a stronghold of the Sarvāstivādins. Thus if the Pali tradition is accepted, one has to assume that during Aśoka's time the Sarvāstivādins confined their main activities mostly around the Mathurā region, the Theravādins around Kauśāmbī and Pāṭaliputra and the Mahāsāṅgikas in Āndhra-deśa. As stated above (p. 98) such a hypothesis runs counter to the findings of the Aśokan inscriptions, which postulate all the time a unified *saṅgha*. Both literary as well as epigraphical data can, however, be made complimentary to each other if it is assumed that what Aśoka attempted was a loose unification of the divergent groups on the grounds of the basic teachings of Buddha—on the basis of the *summum bonum* of Buddhist religion without laying undue emphasis on the *vinaya* rules or any uniform code of behaviour. In the Bairat edict Aśoka possibly intended to drive at the basic concepts of Buddha's teachings. The attempted unification, then, laid emphasis on the ideology rather than on the practices that might have varied from sect to sect, from region to region, thereby also affording free scope to accommodate the structural innovations set afloat by Aśoka himself.

Yet the absence of name of any sect in Aśoka's inscriptions is puzzling. Does it mean that the Buddhist church was not then so much divided despite differences of opinion amongst the followers stationed at various widely-separated places? Surprisingly, no epigraphical evidence on the presence of sects even during the second century

[1] N. Dutt, *op. cit*, (1945), p. 252 writes, 'The *Saṅghatthera* of Pāṭaliputra is called in the Sanskrit texts as Yaśas while in Pāli, it is Yonaka Dhammarakkhita. Prominence is given to Upagupta of Mathurā in the Sanskrit traditions and Moggaliputta Tissa in Pāli. This is evidently a result of the sectarian bias. Upagupta was a Sarvāstivādin and so he is mentioned in the Sanskrit texts belonging to the Sarvāstivādins. He is ignored in the Theravāda tradition preserved in Pāli, which puts up the name of Moggaliputta Tissa instead. Both Upagupta and Moggaliputta Tissa might be historical persons, but their position as a religious adviser of Aśoka should be discounted.' It seems, however, quite likely that the Theravādins, with their main sphere of activity around the royal capital enjoyed certain privileges over the others stationed at far-off places.

B.C., when *stūpas* of Bharhut, Sanchi, Amaravati and Bodh-Gaya came into existence, is available; equally doubtful is the occurrence of similar references in the inscriptions of the first century B.C. It is generally believed that the Kāśyapīyas are referred to in the Pabhosa cave-inscription datable to the second-first century B.C. but the restoration of the name *Kasapiya* is doubtful.[1] Further, this sect which branched out of the Sarvāstivādins could hardly come into prominence in the Kauśāmbī region, then a centre of the Theravādins. The evidence in hand, therefore, justifies the postulation that no sect is specifically mentioned in the inscriptions of the second-first century B.C. Perhaps the earliest mention of names of sects is in the Mathurā lion pillar-capital inscription now generally ascribed to the beginning of the first century A.D.; in fact, one finds several inscriptional evidence on the existence of sects during the period in different parts of India too. On the other hand, it has to be acceded that sectarian division in the Buddhist church started much earlier. This anomaly cannot easily be explained unless it is assumed that the sectarian bias was neither much well-defined till that time nor was it allowed to come out in public. Only after the construction of the *stūpas* of Bharhut, Amaravati etc., when Buddhist ideas and birth-legends caught the imagination of the populace that amorphous groups might have begun asserting their individuality in the open.

In the inscriptions of the first century one finds the mention of at least two sects, viz., the Sarvāstivādins and the Mahāsāṅghikas. While the names of the former occur in the inscriptions of Taxila, Mathurā, Śrāvastī and Sarnath, all ascribable to the first century A.D., those of the latter are mentioned in the inscriptions of Karle and Mathurā. A perusal of epigraphical data reveals the interesting fact that by about the second-third century A.D. different branches of the Mahāsāṅghikas came to limelight in the Deccan yielding their places in the north and north-west India to the Sarvāstivādins or their offshoots. That the Mahāsāṅghikas had their footholds in the extreme north-west may be affirmed by the Wardak vase inscription (above, p. 72). It is, however, certain that the supremacy of the Mahāsāṅghikas in the lower Deccan remained unchallenged for a long time.

As indicated above (p. 99) the Mahāsāṅghikas might have spread to Āndhra-deśa during the Maurya occupation of the region. Some very faint indication on their presence at Amaravati by about the second century B.C. comes from the recently-discovered stele wherein emphasis is laid on Buddha's association with several Vaiśālī scenes (also, p. 5); the Vajjian monks forming the nucleus of the Mahāsāṅghika sect should normally strive to cast a halo around their place of origin. Further, the formation of *goshṭhi* or committee[2] for the construction of *stūpas* at Amaravati and Bhattiprolu is also reminiscent of a democratic spirit which the original Mahāsāṅghika sect possibly imbibed from the Vajjian republic. Besides these indirect proofs, there is as yet no direct

[1] D. C. Sircar, *op. cit.*, p. 96. According to him the last letter is certainly *tra*.

[2] A. Ghosh and H. Sarkar, *op. cit.*, The word *goshṭhī* occurs not only at Amaravati (*Dhaṁñekad Vaṁda-nāma goṭhi*) and Bhattiprolu (*Ep. Ind.*, II, pp. 327-29) but also in one of the Sanch inscriptions (*ibid.*, pp. 99-102).

inscriptional evidence suggesting the presence of the Mahāsāṅghikas in Āndhra-deśa; however, this sect must have had a settlement at Karle in the first century A.D.

Of the offshoots of the Mahāsāṅghikas, the Chaityakas undoubtedly held their supremacy in the Amaravati region during the second century, for an inscription of the time of Vāsishṭhīputra Pulumāyi (A.D. 135-163) clearly refers to their settlement at the *mahā-chaitya* at Amaravati (*mahāchetiye Chetikiyānam nikāsa parigahe*).[1] Apart from the Chaityakas or Chetiyavādakas the inscriptions from Amaravati mention the name of another sect, the Mahāvanaseliyas, which also flourished some time in the second century.[2] As the Chaityakas had already settled down at the *Mahā-chaitya* site, the monastic establishment of the Mahāvanaseliyas might have been situated elsewhere. It was possibly the Chaityakas who renovated the *stūpa* at Amaravati by the second century A.D., and also introduced, though on a limited scale, the image of Buddha on the drum-slabs. Perhaps the *āyaka*-platforms to the *stūpa* were also added in the same period. Regarding the settlement of the Mahāvanaseliyas the evidence is absolutely meagre but for its clear reference in an inscription.[3] In all likelihood the influence of the Chaityakas crossed the limit of Āndhra-deśa to reach as far west as Nasik where one Mugūdāsa belonging to the lay-community of Chetikas i.e., Chaityakas (*Chētika-upāsakiya*) donated a cave for use as the residence of the monks.[4] But the sphere of activity of the Mahāvanaseliyas remained confined possibly to Amaravati in spite of the fact that their western branch known as Apara-mahāvina-seliyas, rose to great prominence at Nagarjunakonda during the third century, Nagarjunakonda being situated actually to the west of Amaravati.[5] It has already been shown that the Aparā-mahāvina-seliyas did not in the beginning subscribe to the idea of image worship nor was the concept of shrine acceptable to them (above, p. 76). This evidence, incidentally, is likely to throw some light on the character of monastic settlement owned by the Mahāvanseliyas; most likely this sect did not also accept the twin ideas of image and the shrine. The absence of any chapel, either apsidal or quadrangular, at Amaravati may likewise show that even the Chaityakas, notwithstanding their belief in the representation of image of the Master, had no liking for the concept of shrine. Eventually Apara-mahāvina-seliyas, as shown earlier (p. 77), yielded not only to the idea of image-worship but also of shrines meant either for the *stupa* or for the image of Buddha. The circumstances which led to

1 C. Sivaramamurti, *Amaravati Sculptures in the Madras Government Museum* (Madras, 1956), pp. 283-84.

2 *Ibid.* pp. 279, 283-84, 289 and 293. The Mahāvanaseliyas are mentioned in the inscriptions of Sivaramamurti's Period II of Amaravati, while the Chaityakas or Chetiyavādakas both in the Periods II and III.

3 J. Burgess, *The Buddhist stūpas of Amaravati and Jaggayyapeta* (London, 1887), p. 105. The inscription begins with *Sidham namo (Bha) gavato achar (iyana) Mahavanasaliyana. . . . .*

4 Lüders' list, no. 1130.

5 How far this postulation is correct cannot be said with certainty but the name Mahāvana-seliyas (Sanskrit Mahāvana-śaila) does not differ in the least from the Apara-mahāvina-seliya (Sanskrit Apara-mahāvana-śaila) but for the prefix *apara* which may mean either 'western' or 'other' branch of the Mahavanaseliya sect.

these changes are not clearly known; an attempt is, however, made below to trace the line of development.

At the risk of reiteration let it be mentioned here that the idea of Buddha image originated either in Gandhāra or in the Mathurā region some time in the first century A.D. Also the concept of apsidal or circular shrines evolved earlier outside Āndhradeśa. Hence, what the Apara-mahāvina-seliyas did in their later days at Nagarjunakonda was to absorb certain trends already in vogue either in western Deccan or in Gandhāra. Of the two trends the Chaityakas of Amaravati had already accepted the concept of Buddha-image,[1] and the idea must have lost its novelty when the Apara-mahāvina-seliyas incorporated it in their creed and practices. And undoubtedly the Chaityakas of Amaravati derived the idea of image-worship from Gandhāra or Mathurā region though they had already formulated the supramundane conception of Buddha.

The apsidal or oblong shrines of Nagarjunakonda might have been inspired either by Gandhāra or by a tradition prevalent in the west coast, the latter appears to be a greater probability because the concept of shrine reached its maturity there, and further, the political condition of the time drew both the coasts culturally to much closer ties. But the influence of Gandhāra in the Buddhist architecture is clearly manifest in the use of wheel-shaped plan, quadrangular monastery, *stūpa* built on high platform, in image-chapels and also possibly in the practice of offering votive-*stūpas*.

The Bahuśrutīya sect of Nagarjunakonda followed more or less the same pattern; and this sect along with the most popular sect, the Apara-mahāvina-seliyas, put into shade all other branches of the Mahāsāṅghikas. Whether any other sect of this school attained popular recognition during the second-third century A.D. is difficult to say. It seems that the Apara-śailas and Pūrva-śailas came into existence in subsequent times possibly in the fourth-fifth centuries A.D., for Hiuen Tsang saw both the settlements in ruins, also thereby indicating their last position in the sequence.[2] But the mention of Pūrva-śailas in one of the Nagarjunakonda inscriptions may indicate that the nucleus of at least the Pūrva-śailas existed by about the third century A.D.[3] Dutt has tried to prove that the inscriptions of Amaravati, Jaggayyapeta and Nagarjunakonda contain references to other sects like the Ayira-haghāna, Rājagiri-nivāsika, Sidhathikā etc.[4] These names do not possibly suggest sects as, (i) the first-mentioned term is an oft-repeated phrase meaning *saṅgha* of the noble; (ii) the second phrase, if viewed in the context, means nothing but a resident of Rajagiri while Sidhathikā is a

[1] Buddha image occurs in the second period of Amaravati according to Sivaramamurti's (*op. cit.*, p. 29) chronology.

[2] 'At a hill to the east of the capital was monastery called *Fu-po-shih-lo* (Pūrvaśilā) or 'East Mountain' and at a hill to the west of the city was the *A-fa-lo-shih-lo* (Avaraśilā) or 'West Mountain' monastery.' See Watters, *op. cit.* p. 214.

[3] J. Ph. Vogel, *op. cit.*, 22. The inscription mentions: *Puvasele taḷākam a* [*laṁ*] *dā ma* [*ṁ*] *ḍavo cha*.

[4] N. Dutt (1945), *op. cit.*, p. 52.

personal name. Excluding all these doubtful cases one may say that at least four sects, viz., the Chaityakas, the Mahāvanaseliyas, the Apara-mahāvina-seliyas, and the Bahuśrutīyas sprang out of the main stem of the Mahāsāṅghikas in Āndhra-deśa by the second-third centuries A.D. Side by side the Mahīśāsakas and the Mahā-vihāra-vāsins, a Theravādin sect from Ceylon, also gained popularity particularly in the Nagarjunakonda area (above, p. 95). Of the two, the Mahīśāsakas remained all along the true adherents of the orthodox Buddhist teachings; their ideology did not perhaps undergo much change even as late as the time of Toramāṇa (*c.* 500-15 A.D.) as it appears from the Kura stone-inscription.[1]

The Pūrva-śailas and the Apara-śailas which flourished in the Āndhra country, after at least the third-fourth centuries, confined their activities mainly around Amaravati (p. 102). But if the reading of *Chetika* in the inscription no. 14 of cave X (pl. V B) at Ajanta[2] is correct one has to postulate the existence of some Chaityaka sect – most probably Chaitya-śailas of the texts – by about the fifth-sixth centuries in the Ajanta region also. Likewise, the Apara-śailas might also have extended their sphere of influence as far west as Kanheri (below, p. 104).

Like the Mahāsāṅghikas, the Sarvāstivādins in spite of their hold over a large territory suffered usual ramification (above, p. 71). From the beginning of the fourth century their influence began to wane specially with the rise of the Sammitīyas who actually drove the Sarvāstivādins out of Sarnath; the latter had earlier secured their position in the region after ousting the Theravādins.[3] Nonetheless, the Sarvāstivādins by virtue of their contact with several outside cultures contributed greatly to the cause of Buddhist art and ideology as well as to the Buddhist Sanskrit literature. As indicated above (p. 70) it was the Sarvāstivādins who also took initiative in giving the Master an anthropomorphic form.

It appears that during the first three or four centuries from the birth of Christ the Gandhāra-Mathurā on the one hand and Āndhra-deśa on the other played great roles in the development of Buddhist art, architecture and ideology. In both the regions the process of liberalization of the rules of discipline to accommodate various popular trends proceeded more or less on a uniform pattern; and hence, one finds close similarity in the popular conception of Buddhism in both the centres. Even the same trend had its echo in the inscriptions of the west coast where the concept of shrine reached its culmination through a medium of tractable rock. The development in the latter region had two clear-cut phases of intensity, the first covered the period from the second century B.C. to the second-third centuries A.D. followed by a period of comparative lull when the centre of gravity shifted to the east coast, and then, came the period of final outbrust. In the first phase the rock-cut architecture was primarily influenced by the idea of *stūpa*-shrine; the scenes from Buddha's life were hardly portrayed even by means of aniconic symbols and the sculptural art in the form of

[1] G. Bühler, 'The new inscription of Toramana Shaha', *Epigraphia Indica*, I, pp. 238-41.
[2] G. Yazdani, *Ajanta*, pt. III (Oxford, 1946), text, p. 93.
[3] N. Dutt (1945), *op. cit.*, pp. 174-75.

exterior embellishment had little didactic or religious strain compared to the art of Bharhut, Sanchi and the earliest phase of Amaravati. At Bhaja, Karle, Pitalkhora and Kondane the underlying theme of the meagre plastic representations comprised mainly the material life: the dancing couples of Karle, the smiling dwarf of Pitalkhora and the Jātaka scenes painted in caves 9 and 10 (pl. VB) at Ajanta are some of the highlights of artistic achievements of the first phase. In this period Buddha was hardly shown in human form notwithstanding its comparatively earlier occurrence at Devnimori, Gujarat, where images of Buddha bear indelible stamp of the Gandhāra tradition.[1]

Unfortunately nothing is known about the sects responsible for such fine architectural and artistic creation: Bhaja, Ajanta, Pitalkhora and Kondane are devoid of reference to any name of sects whereas Karle, Kanheri, Nasik and Junnar have brought to light names of at least five sects, e.g. the Mahāsāṅghikas (Lüders' nos. 1105-06), the Dharmōttarīyas (Lüders' nos. 1094-95 and 1152), the Bhadrāyaṇīyas (Lüders' nos. 987, 1018 and 1123-24), the Chaityakas (Lüders' nos. 1130) and the Apara-śailas.[2] Some authorities have read the name of another sect, the Aparājitas, in the inscriptions from Junnar caves,[3] but Buddhist texts do not mention any such schools. Karle appears to have been the seat of the Mahāsānghikas, while Nasik and Junnar had respectively the settlements of the Bhadrāyaṇīyas and the Dharmōttarīyas, the last-mentioned sect had also an establishment at Sūrpāraka, modern Sopara (Lüders' list nos. 1094-95 from Karle). The name of another sect, the Chaityakas, also occurs in one of the Nasik inscriptions yet the purport of the epigraph does not suggest the existence of a school; the reference to the Dharmōttarīyas in two Karle inscriptions does not also imply the presence of any settlement there belonging to this sect. But undoubtedly the Bhadrāyaṇīyaṣ had another settlement at Kanheri, thereby suggesting that this sect like the Dharmōttarīyas had a large number of followers in western India during the first-second centuries. Evidently, the Mahāsāṅghikas had to face a strong opposition in the upper Deccan in extending their sphere of influence.

Very little information in respect of the doctrines of the Dharmōttarīyas and Bhadrāyaṇīyas is available in the texts; Dutt is of the opinion that their views were very near to the Sammitīyas, whose popularity rose to great height during Harshavardhana's time (606-647 A.D.).[4] One of the earliest reference to the Sammitīyas comes from a Gupta inscription at Sarnath which records the fact that by 300 A.D. this sect drove the Sarvāstivādins out of Sarnath (above, p. 103). It is, therefore, evident that the Sammitīyas attained popularity only in the fourth century though their allied schools carved out for themselves important positions much earlier in the west coast. Further, the concept of image-worship formed an integral

1 *Indinn Archaeology 1961-62—A Revicw*, pp. 12-13.

2 M.G. Dikshit, 'A new Buddhist sect at Kanheri' *Indian Historical Quarterly*, XVIII (1942), pp. 60-63.

3 Lüders' list, nos. 1158 and 1163.

4 N. Dutt (1945); *op. cit.*, p. 174.

part of the Sammitīya doctrine whereas the Dharmōttarīyas and the Bhadrāyaṇīyas did not subscribe to this change at least upto the second century A.D. It is, however, certain that the concept of shrine, mostly apsidal on plan, reached its perfection at the hands of at least the two last-mentioned sects of the west coast. (For distribution of apsidal *stūpa*-shrines in India see p. 30 and fig. 27).

According to Dutt the monks belonging to the schools of Vajjiputtakas or Vāśīputrīyas, Dharmōttarīyas, Bhadrāyaṇīyas, Chhannagarikas and Sammitīyas 'were probably those Vajjiputtakas who submitted to the decisions of the Second Council and gave up their heresies as distinguished from those who preferred to remain apart and form a distinct *saṅgha* of their own.'[1] In fact, the Sarnath inscription clearly states Sammitīyas as belonging to the Vātsīputrikas.[2] The Sammitīyas are also sometimes called Āvantaka, for the school owed its origin to Mahākachchāyana, the famous monk of Avantī; this tradition thus connects the Sammitīyas and their cognate schools also with the Theravādins. Incidentally, the fact that Dhammarakkhita, a *Yavana*, was sent to Aparānta also suggests that the first wave of Buddhism in the west coast had a Theravāda substratum (above, p. 99). All this may show that, in the beginning, the Dharmōttarīyas and Bhadrāyaṇīyas were remotely connected with the Theravāda school, and perhaps both developed their own ideology to suit the conditions prevalent in their respective areas. Basically they were Hīṇayānists believing only in the worship of *stūpa* enshrined in a chapel. Yet they did not forget altogether the memorial aspect of the *stūpa*, for miniature *stūpas* raised in honour of leading monks appears to be a common practice noticed at sites like Bhaja,[3] Bedsa[4] and Pitalkhora.[5]

When the above-mentioned Buddhist schools of the northern Deccan took to image-worship is, however, not known but it is fairly certain that the first structural activity of the west coast was not generally concerned with the installation of the Buddha-icon. On the other hand, the Sammitīyas certainly believed in the worship of image, besides accepting the theory of *pudgala* or 'individual personality'; possibly they too subscribed to the concept of shrine. The Dharmōttarīyas and the Bhadrāyaṇīyas though accepting the latter aspect desisted the idea of representing Buddha in anthropomorphic from till at least the second-third centuries A.D. But the history of these sects after second-third centuries A.D. is absolutely blank, nor it is known for certain if any other sect spread to northern Deccan and eclipsed their popularity. There are some evidence, as given below, to show that northern Deccan drew its inspiration so far as the worship of image is concerned primarily from Mathurā or Sarnath, and not much from the lower Deccan, at least in the beginning of the new movement. At the

[1] N. Dutt (1945), *op. cit.*, p. 174.

[2] J. Ph. Vogel, 'Epigraphical Discoveries at Sarnath,' *Epigraphia Indica,* VIII, p. 172. The inscription runs as *A (cha) ryyanaṁ Sa(mmi)tiyanaṁ parigraha Vātsīputrikānam.*

[3] Lüders' list, nos. 1080-82.

[4] *Ibid.*, no. 1110.

[5] Like one of the caves at Bhaja, cave 11 of Pitalkhora contains three *stūpas,* thus indicating the prevalence of an identical custom.

same time, it has to be borne in mind that in view of the popularity of the worship of image in different parts of India the evidence of some sporadic attempts on the part of certain section of monks or lay-worshippers to introduce the icon of Buddha prior to the second phase may as well come to light, but these attempts could not have assumed any proportions so as to take the form of a movement.

An examination of the cave-inscriptions from western India reveals that a group of monks, styled in the epigraphs as *Śākya-bhikshu*, made its presence felt in the northern Deccan by donating liberally the image of Buddha. That these monks had their main sphere of influence in the north, specially around Sarnath and Mathurā, is evident from the inscriptions, mostly datable to the Gupta period, discovered at Mathurā, Kasia, Deoriya and Sarnath.[1] Like friar Bala these *Śākya-bhikshus* were mainly interested in offering the image of Buddha to different Buddhist *saṅgha.* In western India monks and nuns of this community made gifts of Buddha-image mostly at Kuda, Kanheri and Ajanta, the last-mentioned place yielding no less than a dozen inscriptions variously from caves II, IX, X, XVI, XXII and XXVI.[2] Taken collectively the names of *Śākya-bhikshus* occurring in the epigraphs of northern Deccan do not substantially differ from those of Mathurā or Sarnath. It is worth while to mention here certain characteristics of the names so that one can easily visualize the oneness of this community of monks. More than two dozen names are known from the inscriptions belonging to different parts of India, yet there is not a single case of repetition of any name though one can at the same time discern certain common links in the names of different individuals. Most likely these names—these appear to be the names conferred by the *saṅgha*—in the majority of the cases followed a definite pattern. For instance, all the available names may be divided into nine broad groups, viz., names starting with (i) Buddha, (ii) Bodhi, (iii) Bhadra, (iv) Bandu, (v) Dharma, (vi) Dhana, (vii) Dṛiḍa, (viii) Saṅgha and (ix) miscellaneous names like Suvīra, Yasadina, Keśava, Brahmosoma and Vyāghrakā (nun). There are five varieties in the group starting with the prefix 'Buddha': Buddhagupta, Buddhasena, Buddhaghosha, Buddhasiṅgha and Buddhapriya. Similarly four varieties with the prefix 'Saṅgha'—Saṅgharakshita, Saṅghadeva, Saṅghapriya and Saṅghagupta—are known. All this evidence may suggest that the *Śākya-bhikshus* formed a compact group by itself with a central *saṅgha* guiding the activities of the individual monks stationed in different parts of India.

It may be argued that *Śākya-bhikshus* need not be distinguished as a distinct group of monks. But in the votive inscriptions from Mathurā and Sarnath the *Śākya-bhikshus* have always been differentiated from ordinary monks or *bhikshus.* A study of the Buddhist votive records, as given by Lüders in his list (nos. 125-49) shows that in the majority of the cases the Buddhist monks are referred to simply as *bhikshus* while the

[1] Lüders' list, nos. 134, 146-149 from Mathurā; 911 from Deoriya; 929[e], 929[j] 929[m], 929[r], 929[t] from Sarnath; 937[a] from Kasia; 989, 990, 1043, 1044, 1046, 1947 from Kanheri and Kuda.

[2] Jas. Burgess and Bhagwanlal Indraji, *Inscriptions from the cave-temples of western India* (Bombay, 1881) pp. 76-88. Also Yadzani *op. cit.*, II to IV, chapters on inscriptions.

term *Śākya-bhikshu* occurs only in five inscriptions. Moreover no. 134 of Lüders draws a line of distinction between the *bhikshu* Buddharakshita and a *Śākya-bhikshu* whose name is now missing.[1] Even in the Mankuwar inscription of Kumāra Gupta I (448 A.D.), when the term *Śākya-bhikshu* must have attained considerable popularity, a Buddhist monk is referred to simply as a *bhikshu.*[2] On all accounts, these are not accidental references, for the word *Śākya-bhikshu* seems to be of comparatively later origin than the terms *bhikshu*, *śramaṇa*, *sthavira* or *thera*, and *arhat*.

There might be some direct or indirect relationship between the terms *Sākya-muni* and *Śākya-bhikshus*, the former occurs in the Rummindei pillar-inscription of Aśoka (*hida Buddhe jāte Sakya-munī ti*), but Buddhist monks in the Aśokan inscriptions, have invariably been mentioned as *bhikshu* though the word *śramaṇa* occurring in the rock-edicts may vaguely include Buddhist monks as well. But the popularization of the name *Śākya-muni*, obviously a name connected with the clan to which Buddha belonged, owed mostly to the Buddhists of north-west India and the Śaka-dominated Mathurā region. The emergence of the *Śākya-bhikshus* as a distinct group was possibly the outcome of a trend which aimed at popularizing the image of *Śākya-muni* and incidentally, emphasizing the importance of the Śākya-clan. It is only against this background that the oft-quoted passage from the *Bṛihat-Saṁhitā* that the *Śākya-bhikshus* alone are fit to instal and consecrate the image of Buddha as the Magas are for the Sun, the Bhāgavats for Vishṇu, *Sabhashma-dvijas* for Sambhu etc.[3] has to be viewed.

In the light of the above discussion one cannot but come to the conclusion that the *Śākya-bhikshus* made a concerted effort to introduce image-worship amongst the sects settled in different cave-monasteries. They were monks with a distinct entity, with a definite ideal and mission. An inscription from cave XXII of Ajanta expresses the view-point of the *Śākya-bhikshus*: Whoever makes an image of Jina (Buddha) becomes complete in beatitude, auspiciousness, and good qualities, and his splendour is brilliant through virtues, and physical organs, and is delightsome to the eyes.[4] Such enthusiasm on the part of a community of monks to offer or instal Buddha-image over a wide area, including the northern Deccan, might have considerably shaped the pattern of the new artistic movement, which not only popularized the anthropomorphic form of Buddha but also the oblong shrines already in vogue in different parts of India including those at Kuda.

As these *Śākya-bhikshus* had their centres at Sarnath and Mathurā many artistic and architectural features might have travelled from these regions to the northern

[1] Lüders' list, no. 134.

[2] D. C. Sircar, *op. cit.*, p. 287.

[3] *Brihatsaṁhita*, S. Dvivedi's edition, ch. 59, v. 19.
Vishṇorbhāgavatān magāṁścha savituḥ śambhoḥ sabhasmadvijān |
Mātṛriṇāmapi maṇḍalakramavido viprān vidurbrahmaṇaḥ ||
Śākyān sarvahitasya śāntamanaso nagnān jinānāṁ vidu-|
Rye yaṁ devamupāśritāḥ svavidhinā taistasya kāryā kriyā ||

[4] Burgess and Bhagwanlal Indraji, *op. cit.*, p. 80.

Deccan; the trend combined with the mature art-tradition of the lower Krishna valley gave rise to a new movement. This new trend had a definite Mahāyānic[1] orientation, for the idea of Bodhisattva-hood of the Mahāyānists, which postulates every being as a potential Buddha, had its full growth in the later periods of Ajanta. In course of time, the concepts of shrine and the worship of image reached their fullness at the hands of west Indian artists, sculptors and architects. Almost an identical process of development resulting in the emergence of the temples like that of Bodh-Gaya and Nalanda could be traced in eastern India.

A critical study of the process of development of the Buddhist ideology may thus show that the idea of shrine, image and in certain cases, the concept of Bodhi tree and railings, apart from the *stūpa*-cult, spread by and by in different parts of India in varying degrees but ultimately the image enshrined in a chapel became the primary attraction in a Buddhist establishment. The Sarvāstivādins in Gandhāra, the Mahāsāṅghikas and their offshoots in the east coast and the Vajjiputtakas and their allied school in the northern Deccan and eastern India accepted this temple-concept in some period of their history or the other; on the other hand, the traits evolved out of some primitive Indian traditions like the *stūpa*-cult or tree-worship receded more and more in the background.

Thus the concept of shrine and worship that ushered in during Aśoka's time inside the Buddhist *saṅgha* eventually reached their culmination in different parts of India and amongst various sects. *Stūpas*, also popularized by Aśoka, were no longer conceived simply as memorials, neither as aniconic symbol of the Master, nor even as the main object of worship. Attempts to represent Buddha in aniconic or in theriomorphic forms assumed wide vogue during the Śuṅga-Sātavāhana period but subsequent history of Buddhist art shows that these trends, though representing several indigenous elements, had a limited role to play and those too, generally as subsidiary decorative motifs. It may also be mentioned here that the theriomorphic representation of Buddha —the idea evidently taken from primitive practices then prevalent in India—also began possibly from the time of Aśoka as, besides the sculptural representation of elephant representing Buddha at Kalsi (pl. XII B) and Dhauli, the Girnar rock-edict mentions specifically the word *śveta-hastī* or 'white elephant'.[2] An urge on the part of Aśoka to represent Gautama Buddha in conceivable form, a form also easily recognized by the general people, was thus manifest in such attempts.

1 An inscription from cave XXII at Ajanta possibly refers to the Mahāyāna doctrine *(Mahāyāna-yāyinaḥ)*. See Yazdani, *op. cit.*, IV, p. 112. An inscription on the pedestal of the image of Khasarpaṇa Lokanāth, of the tenth-eleventh centuries, mentions the name of one Īśvarasiṁha as a follower of Mahāyāna doctrine. See Nalini Kanta Bhattasali, *Iconography of Buddhist and Brahmanical Sculptures in the Dacca Museum* (Dacca, 1929), pp. 25-26.

2 Girnar rock-edict mentions . . . . *rva-sveto hasti sarva-loka-sukhāharo nama* (' . . . the entirely white elephant bringing indeed happiness to the whole world') below the now-missing elephant representing Buddha. The world *gajatame* ('the best elephant') occurs below the figure of a carved elephant at Kalsi also. Viewed in this context the phrase *hasti dasaṇā* of the Fourth Rock-Edict of Aśoka appears quite significant.

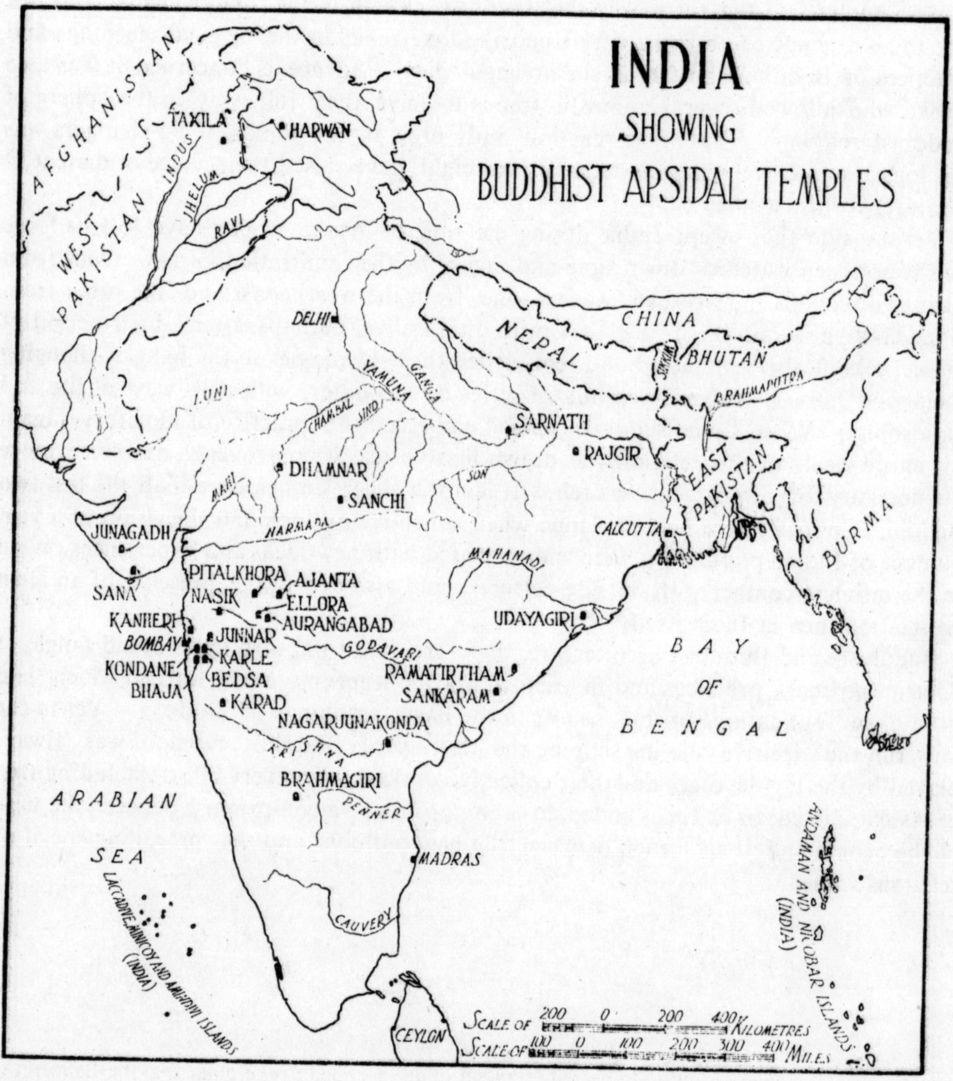
INDIA
SHOWING
BUDDHIST APSIDAL TEMPLES
AFGHANISTAN
TAXILA
HARWAN
INDUS
JHELUM
RAVI
WEST PAKISTAN
DELHI
CHINA
NEPAL
BHUTAN
SIKKIM
BRAHMAPUTRA
YAMUNA
GANGA
LUNI
CHAMBAL
SIND
SARNATH
RAJGIR
EAST PAKISTAN
DHAMNAR
SON
MAHI
SANCHI
BURMA
NARMADA
JUNAGADH
CALCUTTA
MAHANADI
PITALKHORA
AJANTA
SANA
NASIK
ELLORA
AURANGABAD
KANHERI
JUNNAR
UDAYAGIRI
BOMBAY
BAY
OF
BENGAL
KONDANE
KARLE
GODAVARI
BHAJA
BEDSA
RAMATIRTHAM
SANKARAM
KARAD
NAGARJUNAKONDA
KRISHNA
BRAHMAGIRI
ARABIAN
SEA
PENNER
MADRAS
ANDAMAN AND NICOBAR ISLANDS (INDIA)
LACCADIVE, MINICOY AND AMINDIVI ISLANDS (INDIA)
CAUVERY
CEYLON
SCALE OF 200 0 200 400 KILOMETRES
SCALE OF 100 0 100 200 300 400 MILES

FIG. 27

Also, the seed that was sown by Aśoka in the third century B.C., so far as the concept of shrine is concerned, had its full growth in subsequent times when Buddha was given a visual human form like any other deity to be adored and worshipped in temples.

Who knows that the turmoil in the Buddhist church in the time of Aśoka was not due to an attempt to absorb alien or unorthodox trends in the original teachings and practices of Buddha? So far as the archaeological evidence is concerned it was also Aśoka who allowed several animistic trends to have their full sway in the sphere of Buddhist religion. That some reaction must brew in the minds of no-changers was but logical and it was those adherents who might have raised their voice of dissent in whatever form that may be.

Yet the tide that swept India during the time of Aśoka would have lost its force had it not been watered down time and again by the infiltration of new ideas from various directions. Two such waves—one from the west coast and the other from Gandhāra—not only kept the Aśokan tradition alive, perhaps after a brief period of quiscence, but also readjusted and remodelled these ideologies in the light of changing social and cultural values born out of series of encounters with new ways of life and philosophy. When some Buddhist *saṅgha* embraced the practice of idolatory, again the entire world of this religion was drawn in a vortex of controversy, and once more the necessity for adjustment was felt. It is not a sheer coincidenee that the last two Buddhist Councils were held at a time when collective outlook and the vision of a vast number of Indian population were impregnated with new ideas and experiences owing to the intimate contact with outside cultures, and also due to the presence of an alien population then in India itself.

Buddhism and Buddhist architecture, therefore, had to absorb in its broad tangle of doctrines, rituals, practices and in architectural conceptions many a trend which had little or no foundation in this soil or in the basic teachings of Buddha. Yet in the long run the decisive role in shaping the destiny of Buddhist religion was always played by the lay-devotees and their collective outlook, for every effort including that of Aśoka, aimed, or at times ended, at a compromise—a compromise between the urge of the people and their ideals, between the new outlook and the prevailing social or religious values.[1]

[1] It is evident from a recently-discovered fragment of an inscribed *āyaka*-pillar that the Bahuśrutīya sect had an establishment at Kesanapalli in District Guntur some time in the middle of the third century A.D. Information from Shri Abdul Waheed Khan, Director of Archaeology and Museums, Andhra Pradesh, Hyderabad, Kesanapalli, as the recent explorations revealed, had a very early phase too, for some of the inscriptions recovered from the site are ascribable, on palaeographic grounds, to the second century B.C. Evidently, its early phase was more or less contemporaneous with that of Amaravati.

SELECT BIBLIOGRAPHY

Annual Reports of the Archaeological Survey of India.

Bapat, P.V., *Two Thousand Five Hundred Years of Buddhism*, New Delhi, 1959.

Barrett, Douglas, *Sculptures from Amaravati in the British Museum*, London, 1954.

Barua, Benimadhab, *Barhut*, 3 vols., Calcutta, 1937.

Barua, Benimadhab, *Gayā and Buddha-Gayā*, 2 vols, Calcutta, 1931 and 1934.

Bhandarkar, D.R., *Asoka*, Calcutta, 1955.

Brown, Percy, *Indian Architecture* (Buddhist and Hindu Periods), Bombay, 1956.

Burgess, James, *Report on the Antiquities in the Bidar and Aurangabad Districts*, Archaeological Survey of Western India, III, London, 1878,

Burgess, James, *Report on the Buddhist Cave Temples and their Inscriptions*, Archaeological Survey of Western India, IV, London, 1883.

Burgess, James, *The Buddhist Stūpas of Amaravati and Jaggayyapeta in the Krishna District, Madras Presidency*, Archaeological Survey of Western India, VI, London, 1887.

Burgess, James, and Indraji, Bhagwanlal, *Inscriptions from the Cave-Temples of Western India*, Archaeological Survey of Western India, no. 10, Bombay, 1881.

Childers, R.C., *Dictionary of the Pali Language*, London, 1909.

Combaz, G., *L'evolution du stupa en Asie*, Catherine, 1937.

Coomaraswamy, A.K., *History of Indian and Indonesian Art*, London, 1927.

Coomaraswamy, A.K., 'Indian Architectural Terms', *Journal of American Oriental Society*, vol. 48, New Haven, 1928.

Coomaraswamy, A.K., 'Early Indian Architecture', *Eastern Art*, II and III, Philadelphia, 1931-32.

Cowell, E.B., ed., *The Jataka*, London, 1957.

Cunningham, Alexander, *Four Reports made during the years 1862-63-64-65*, Archaeological Survey Report, I and II, Simla, 1871.

Cunningham, Alexander, *Mahābodhi or the Great Buddhist Temple under the Bodhi tree at Buddha-Gaya*, London, 1892.

Cunningham, Alexander, *The Stūpa of Bharhut*, Varanasi, 1962 (reprinted).

Davids, T.W., Rhys, *The Buddhist Suttas*, Sacred Books of the East, XI, Oxford, 1881.

Davids, T.W., Rhys, and Carpenter, J. Estlin, ed., *Sumaṅgala-Vilāsinī*, Pali Text Society, London, 1886.

Davids, T.W., Rhys, and Carpenter, J. Estlin. ed., *Dīgha-Nikāya*, Pali Text Society, London, 1903.

Deshpande, M.N., 'The rock-cut caves of Pitalkhora', *Ancient India*, no. 15, New Delhi, 1959.

Dhavalikar, M.K., *Sanchi: a Cultural Study*, Deccan College Building Centenary and Silver Jubilee Series, no. 42, Poona, 1965.

Dutt, Nalinaksha, *Early Monastic Buddhism*, 2 vols., Calcutta, 1941 and 1945.

Dutt, Nalinaksha, *Aspect of Mahāyāna Buddhism and its relation to Hīnayāna*, London, 1930.

Dutt, Sukumar, *Buddhist Monks and Monasteries of India*, London, 1962.

Epigraphia Indica, I, II, VIII, X, XX, XXI, XXXIII, XXXIV, XXXV and XXXVI.

Feer, M. Leon, *Saṁyutta-Nikāya*, V, *Mahāvagga*, Pali Text Society, London, 1898.

Fergusson, James, and Burgess, James, *The Cave-temples of India*, London. 1880.

Fergusson, James, *A History of Indian and Eastern Architecture*, 2 vols., London, 1910.

Gangoly, O.C., *Indian Architecture*, Bombay, 1946.

Gokhle, B.G., *Asoka and Buddhism*, Baroda, 1948.

Geiger, W., *The Mahāvaṁsa*, Pali Text Society, London, 1912.

Ghosh, A., ed., *Indian Archaeology—A Review*, 1953-54 to 1965-66, published by the Archaeological Survey of India, New Delhi.

Ghosh, A., 'Taxila (Sirkap), 1944-45', *Ancient India*, no. 4, New Delhi, 194.

Ghosh, A., 'Rajgir, 1950', *Ancient India*, no. 7, New Delhi, 1951.

Ghosh, A., *Rajgir*, New Delhi, 1958.

Ghosh, A., ed., *Archaeological Remains Monuments and Museums*, parts I and II, New Delhi, 1964.

Ghosh, A., and Sarkar, H., 'Beginnings of Sculptural Art in south-east India: a stele from Amaravati', *Ancient India*, no. 20, New Delhi, 1966.

Grünwedel, Albert, *Buddhist Art in India*, London, 1901.

Hardy, E., *Aṅguttara-Nikāya*, IV, Pali Text Society, London, 1899.

Hultzsch, E., *Corpus Inscriptionum Indicarum*, I, (Inscriptions of Asoka).

Jones, J.J., *Mahāvastu*, I-IV, London, 1956.

Kane, P.V., *History of Dharmasastra*, IV, Poona, 1953.

Kashyap, Bhikkhu J., *The Chullavagga*, Nalanda-Devanāgarī-Pali-Series, 1956.

Kern, Heinrich, *Manual of Indian Buddhism*, Strassburg, 1896.

Konow, Sten, *Corpus Inscriptionum Indicarum*, vol. II, part (i) (Kharoṣṭhi Inscriptions).

Law, B.C., *Study of Mahāvastu*, Calcutta, 1930.

Longhurst, A.H., *The Buddhist Antiquities of Nagarjunakonda, Madras Presidency*, Memoir of Archaeological Survey of India, no. 54, Delhi, 1938.

Lüders, H., 'A list of Brahmi Inscriptions', *Epigraphia Indica*, vol. X, New Delhi, 1960 (reprinted).

Lüders, H., *Corpus Inscriptionum Indicarum*, II, pt. II (Bharhut Inscriptions), New Delhi, 1965.

Legge, James, *A Record of Buddhist Kingdoms being an account by the Chinese monk Fa-hien of his travels in India and Ceylon (A.D. 399-414)*, Oxford, 1886.

Majumdar, R.C., ed., *The Age of Imperial unity*, History and Culture of the Indian people, II, Bombay, 1954.

Majumdar, R.C. ed., *The Classical Age*, History and Culture of the Indian people, III, Bombay, 1960.

Malalasekera, G.P., *Dictionary of Pāli Proper Names*, 2 vols., London, 1960.

Marshall, John, and others, *Monuments of Sanchi*.

Marshall, John, *Taxila*, 3 vols., Cambridge, 1951.

Mitra, Debala, *Ajanta*, New Delhi, 1965.

Mitra, Debala, *Sanchi*. New Delhi, 1966.

Oldenberg, H., ed., *Vinaya-Piṭaka*, II, *Chullavagga*, Pali Text Society, London, 1880.

Pande, G C., *Studies in the Origins of Buddhism*, Allahabad, 1957.

Ramachandran, T.N., *Nāgārjuṇakoṇḍa 1938*, Mem. of Arch. Surv. of India, no. 71, Delhi, 1953.

Ray, Amita, *Villages, Towns and Secular Buildings in Ancient India* (*c.* 150 B.C.—*c.* 350 A.D.), Calcutta, 1964.

Ray, Nihar Ranjan, *Maurya and Suṅga Art*, Calcutta, 1948.

Rea, A., *South Indian Buddhist Antiquities*, Madras, 1894.

Rowland, Benjamin T., *The Art and Architecture of India*.

Sahni, Daya Ram, *Guide to the Buddhist ruins of Sarnath*, Delhi, 1933.

Sahni, Daya Ram, *Archaeological Remains and Excavations of Bairat*, Jaipur.

Saraswati, S.K., *A Survey of Indian Sculpture*, Calcutta, 1957.

Sarkar, H., 'Some Aspects of the Buddhist Monuments at Nagarjunakonda', *Ancient India*, no. 16, New Delhi, 1962.

Sarkar, H., and Mishra, B.N., *Nagarjunakonda*, New Delhi, 1966.

Sircar, D.C., *Select Inscriptions bearing on Indian History and Civilizations*, I, Calcutta, 1942. Revised edition published in 1966.

Sivaramamurti, C., *Amaravati Sculptures in the Madras Government Museum*, Madras, 1956.

Subrahmanyam, R., *Buddhist Remains in Salihundam*, Hyderabad, 1964.

Takakusu, J., and Nagai, Makoto, ed., *Samantapāsādikā*, London, 1947.

Thomas, L.A., and Thomas, F.W., *The Beginnings of Buddhist Art and other Essays on Indian and Central Asian Archaeology*, Paris, 1917.

Taylor, Arnold C., ed., *Katha-Vatthu*, Pali Text Society, London, 1897.

Watters, Thomas, *On Yuan Chwang's Travels in India (A.D. 629-645)*, Delhi, 1961 (reprinted).

Yazdani, G., *Ajanta*, 4 pts., London, 1930, 1933, 1946 and 1955.

Subrahmanyam, R., *Salihundam, A Buddhist Site in Andhra Pradesh*, Hyderabad, 1964.

INDEX[1]

1 Assistance was received from Srimati Manjusri Sarkar in the preparation of the index.

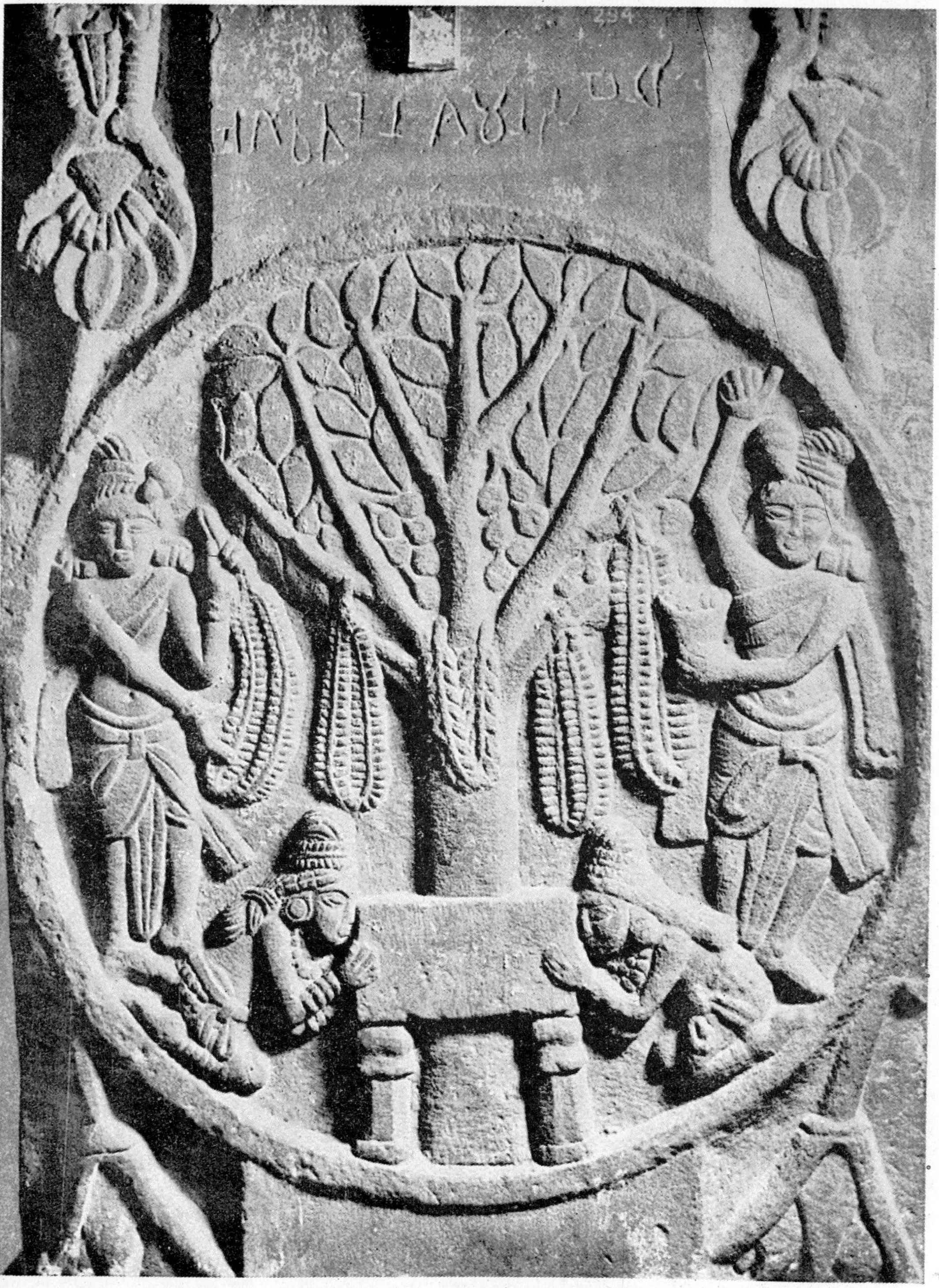

Bharhut : Bodhi tree of Buddha Kanakamuni with label 'Bhagavato Konigamenasa Bodhi'

PLATE II

A

B

Amaravati: inscribed stele, A, *scenes from Vaiśālī, and* B, *Śrāvastī and Jetavana*

A

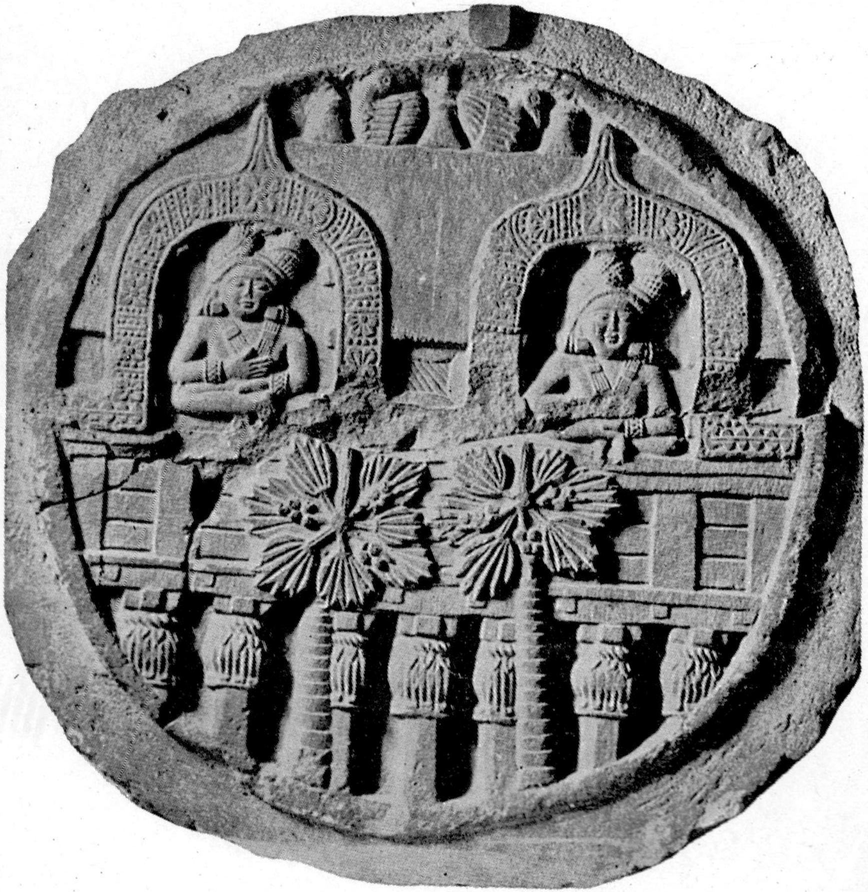

B

Bharhut: A, *Vijayanto pāsāda (top right), and* B, *structure built on columns*

A

B

A, *Sanchi: Brahmanical stūpa;* B, *Nagarjuni Hill: façade of Lomas Rishi cave*

A

B

A, *Salihundam: circular stūpa-shrine;* B, *Ajanta: cave 10, interior view*

A

B

A, *Bhaja: interior of cave;* B, *Karle: interior view of main cave*

A

B

A, *Guntapalli : ribbed ceiling and stūpa below, of circular shrine;* B, *Ajanta : cave 19, with Buddha-figure carved on stūpa*

PLATE VIII

A

B

Nagarjunakonda: A, *Site* 9, *and* B, *Site 24*

A

B

Nagarjunakonda : A, *Site 38*, *and* B, *Site 5*

PLATE X

A

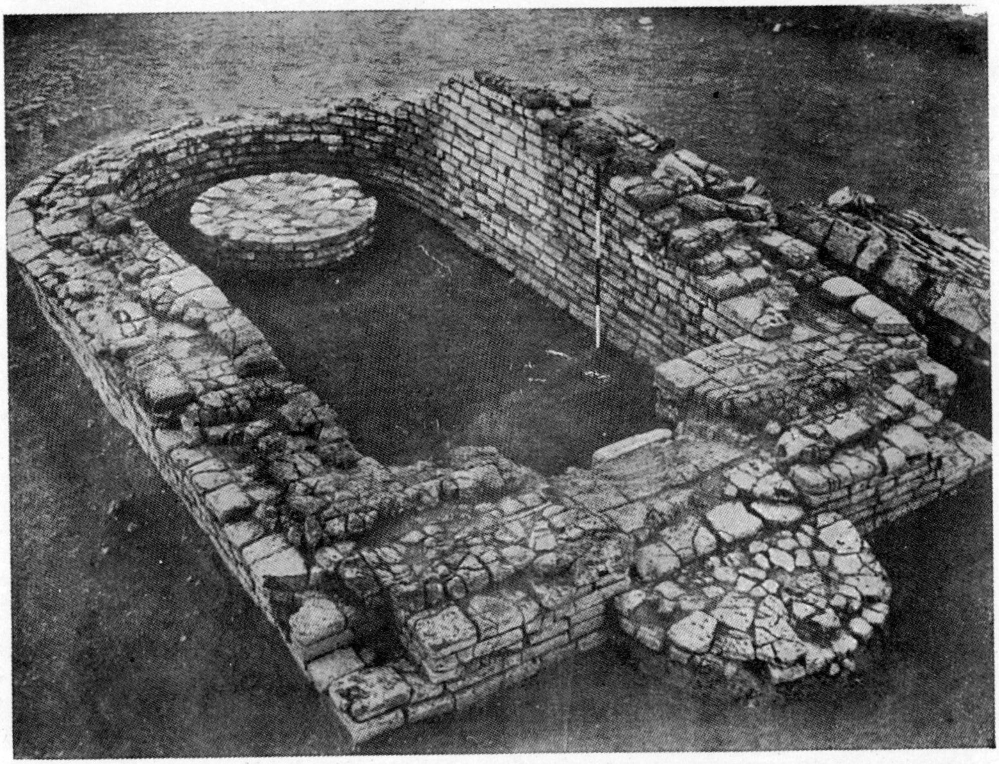

B

Nagarjunakonda : A, *Site 27, and* B, *Site 51*

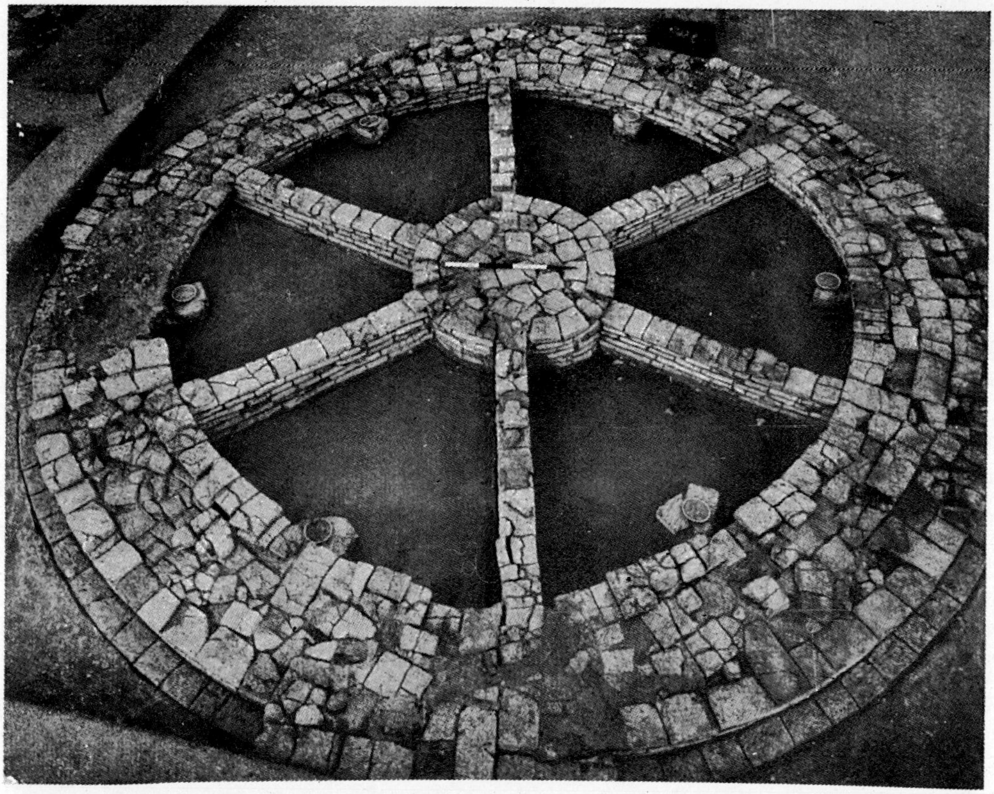

A

B

Nagarjunakonda: A, *Site 30, and* B, *Site 16*

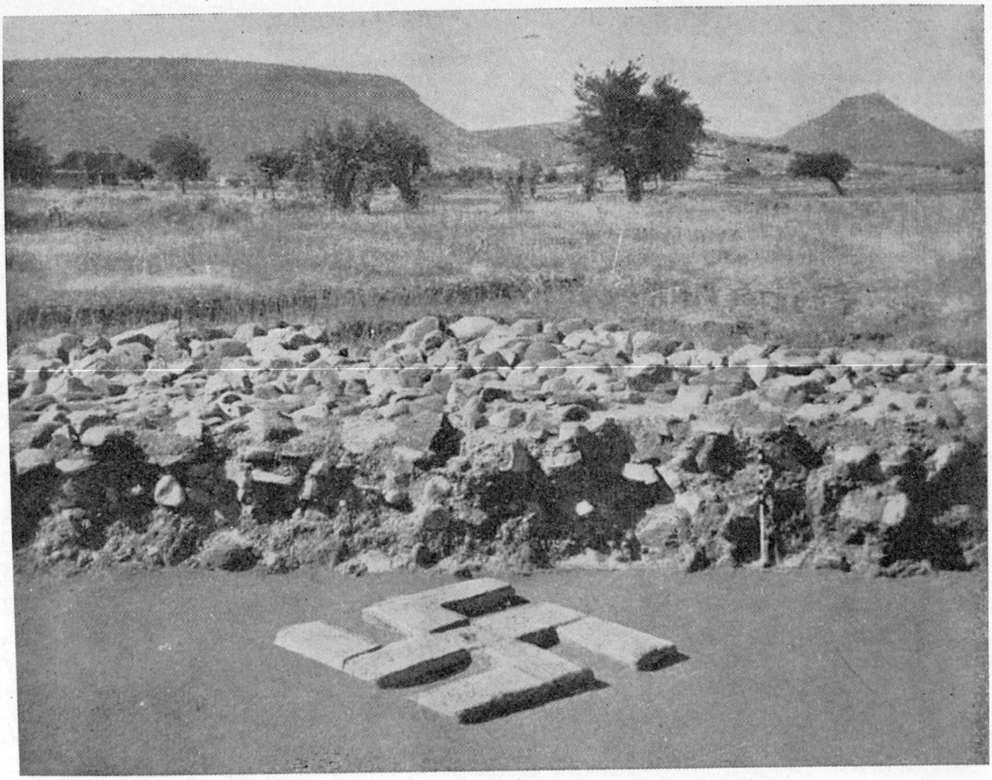

A

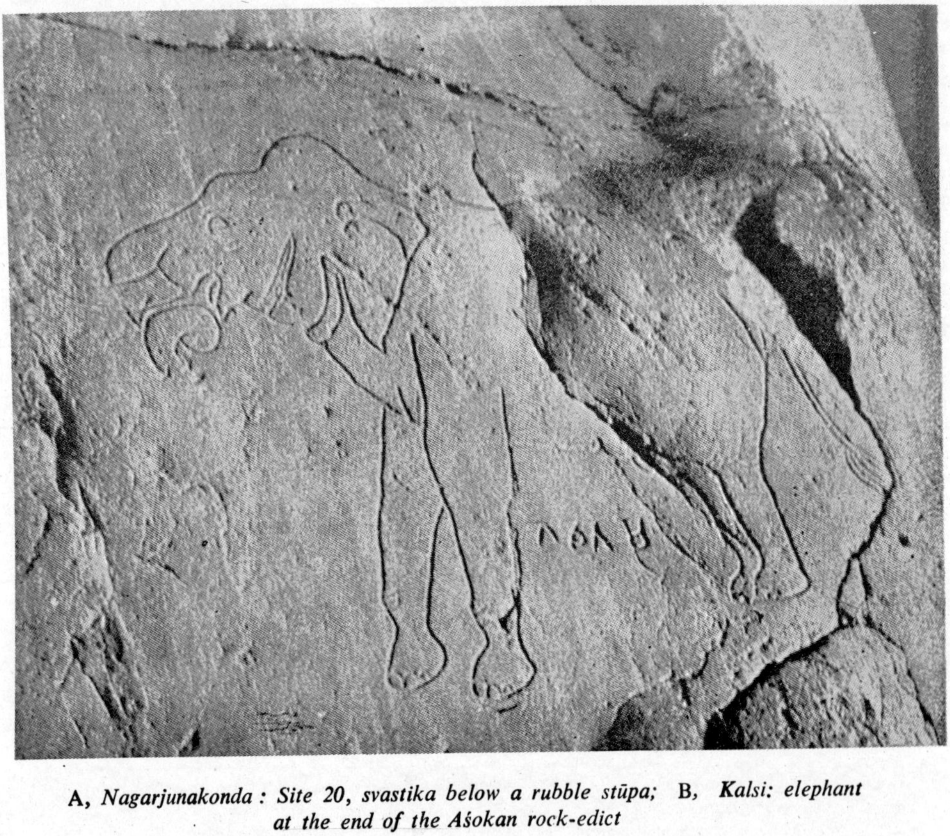

B

A, *Nagarjunakonda : Site 20, svastika below a rubble stūpa;* B, *Kalsi: elephant at the end of the Aśokan rock-edict*